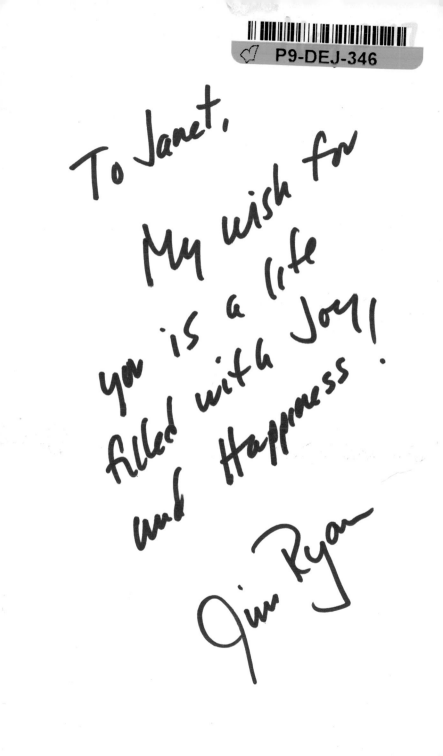

To Janet,

My wish for
you is a life
filled with Joy!
and Happiness!

Jim Ryan

Simple
Happiness

52 Easy Ways to Lighten Up

Simple
Happiness

52 Easy Ways to Lighten Up

"A great book to keep handy as a
reminder of the many things we can do
to feel good everyday!"

Jim Ryan

AuthorHouse™
1663 Liberty Drive, Suite 200
Bloomington, IN 47403
www.authorhouse.com
Phone: 1-800-839-8640

AuthorHouse™ UK Ltd.
500 Avebury Boulevard
Central Milton Keynes, MK9 2BE
www.authorhouse.co.uk
Phone: 08001974150

First published by AuthorHouse 10/30/2006

ISBN: 1-4259-7585-2 (sc)

Layout and Interior Design by the Legwork Team.

Printed in the United States of America
Bloomington, Indiana

This book is printed on acid-free paper.

This book is dedicated to my mother,
Rose Ryan,
whose laughter has always, and still does,
light up our lives.

*In medieval times,
the followers of Saint Francis of Assisi
wanted to know what to do when
they took to the streets.
"Tell everybody about the love of God,"
St. Francis advised.
"If necessary, use words."*

— Excerpt from *The CEO and the Monk:
One Company's Journey to Profit and Purpose*

BY ROBERT B. CATELL, CEO, KEYSPAN,
KENNY MOORE AND GLENN RIFKIN

Contents

ACKOWLEDGEMENTS...10
FOREWORD: By Greg Murphy, Ph.D..............12
INTRODUCTION: Opportunity Knocks 16

CHAPTERS:
THE BASICS
1   You Become What You
     Think About...19
2   Thought Systems 22
3   Your Natural State of Mind................25
4   From Point A to Point B......................29
5   Why You Need Teachers 31
6   When the Student is Ready,
     the Teacher Will Appear 34

THINGS TO THINK ABOUT
7   You Live in a Mansion..........................37
8   What is Compassion?...........................40
9   Are You Really a Creature
     of Habit? 42
10   It's a Long Life 45
11   Are You a Human Doing
     or a Human Being?..............................48
12   Being Prepared is Half the Battle.......50
13   Moods are Not Terminal......................53
14   You've Raised Your Kids, Now All
     You Have To Do is Love Them 56
15   That's All the Lumber You Sent 59
16   Stress is a Choice 61
17   In the Middle of the Difficulty Lies
     Opportunity 66
18   It's All Made Up Anyway.....................69

TAKE A LOOK AT YOURSELF
19   What Makes You Happy?......................71
20   Are Your Antennas Up? 74
21   Who's Responsible? 76
22   Do You Make the Time?........................79
23   Are You Painting the Past Blue? 82
24   Don't Make Assumptions.....................84

THINGS TO DO
25   Appreciate, Appreciate,
     Appreciate..87

26   Follow Your Bliss.................................90
27   Pay It Forward 93
28   Enjoy Creation.....................................95
29   Feed Your Mind 97
30   Volunteer 100
31   Start as Soon as You Wake Up 102
32   Lighten Up 105
33   Don't Be Discouraged........................108
34   Visualize 110
35   You Can Meditate 114
36   The Golden Rule.................................117

STRATEGIES
37   Is Someone Living in Your Head
     Rent Free? 121
38   Have a Healthy Disregard for the
     Good Opinion of Others 123
39   Relax—You May Only Have a
     Few Minutes Left................................126
40   God Loves You as Much as
     He Loves Me.......................................128
41   This is the Day the Lord
     Has Made 130
42   Four Assumptions 132
43   Living in the Present Moment...........135
44   Oops—There You Go Again................140

REACHING HIGHER
45   Be the Compassionate Observer
     of Yourself..143
46   What is Your Mission in Life?..........145
47   Your Greatest Fear or Your
     Greatest Joy.......................................147
48   Believe in Miracles 150
49   Your Spiritual Side—
     You are Not Only Human 153

UNLOCK YOUR POWER
50   Becoming a Little Happier.................157
51   Don't Die with Your
     Music Still in You 160
52   Start to Live "Heaven on Earth" 163

ABOUT THE AUTHOR 166

Acknowledgements

I wish to express sincere thanks to all of those who have played a significant part in the creation of this book—some directly, others indirectly, all invaluable just the same.

Special heartfelt thanks go out to my loving wife, Diane, who remains always unwavering in her support and belief in me to accomplish whatever I put my mind to.

For continuing to push me in this direction for years, I want to thank my long-time friend, Greg Murphy. Greg, I am forever grateful. The time you spent in listening and sharing is what helped me formulate many of the ideas contained in this book. Your psychology wisdom and savvy in its current trends have served to keep my approach realistic and balanced.

Great admiration and appreciation goes to my biggest fan, Dan Murphy, who always saw more in me than I saw in myself. Thanks, Dan.

Much gratitude to all the men at the DWI Alternative Facility in Suffolk County, New York, for their overwhelming positive feedback to my Personal Development Courses; you ignited a spark in me to take my message to the masses.

When my focus needed sharpening or my eyes opened with new ideas, I could always count on my mentor and dear friend, Lee Holcomb. Lee, I will always be grateful for your light.

Many thanks go to Christina Clarke for having the wonderful knack of being able to capture the essence of my entire talks into just a few precise words for my speaking literature.

This book may have been written by hand, the old fashion way, but it took the typing skills of my assistant, Grace Burke, to put my words into digital format. Grace, I am grateful for your enthusiasm, vision and encouragement, all of which motivated me to move this book forward.

I was certainly in the right place at the right time when I bumped into Maggie Kalas, a woman of many talents. Maggie, thanks for not only being the content editor of my book, the creative designer of the book cover, a marketing consultant for my professional speaking, but for being my quasi-spiritual coach along the way. You sure knew how to challenge me to make this book the best it can be.

And, a final thanks to you, the reader, for giving me a chance to make a difference.

Foreword:
Greg Murphy, Ph.D.

As an alternative to studying mental disabilities, recently psychologists have begun to study normal or happy people to understand what factors make them the way they are. Martin Seligman is one of the first psychologists to show interest in investigating what makes people healthy instead of focusing on their deficits. In addition, other psychologists have begun to report on the dynamics of well-functioning social relationships. Another example is the "Positive Behavior Support" approach, which has been implemented in many schools throughout the country in recent years. Results of these programs have helped improve the overall social atmosphere in schools.

Furthermore, psychologists have started to analyze how people can enhance their access to innate resources of joy, compassion and connectedness. This approach or concept has been called "mindfulness." It emphasizes encouraging people to choose helpful responses rather than their old ineffective habits. In my work as a school and clinical psychologist, I have seen many people that have been caught in negative patterns of behavior. Moreover, countless people believe that they can't change their behavior and/or their attitudes. However, the research and my experience clearly show that simply is not the case. People can definitely make significant changes in their behavior for the better.

For the past 35 years as a clinical psychologist, I have successfully applied the principles of positive reinforcement and successive approximation to help people to improve their attitudes and behavior. In that same timeframe, my relationship with Jim Ryan was cultivated by my attraction to and respect for his enthusiastic attitude toward life. It always amazed me how his spirit and exceptional appreciation of nature and people, of which he always makes a point to celebrate, never failed to produce positive results. He lives life with a keen emphasis on family, friends, education, service to others and interests that are rewarding and beneficial. One late August back when he was a young secondary-school French teacher, he told me how excited he was about teaching his classes that September. It seemed that Jim's success in teaching was directly attributed to his cheerful dedication to the craft. At home, his achievements continue with being married to his wife, Diane, for 33 years, raising three children and now enjoying two grandchildren. His warm enthusiasm about being with his family has always been quite remarkable.

Over the years, Jim and I would get together for a round of golf or to play tennis. We would spend hours afterward talking, delving into all aspects of life. Jim never ceased to have illuminating thoughts about personal development and an honest desire to share them with the world. One wonderful idea I recall was about his wanting to help companies to establish an internal framework for implementing viable volunteering programs. My reply to that and to all his inspirations was one of whole-hearted encouragement. "Jim, you should be giving talks; you're a natural," I would say. And he would light up with the possibility of doing it. It prompted me to ask a colleague of mine, who does public speaking, how Jim could get started. One question, he asked me, "What does he want to talk about?" And that was the question I posed to Jim some years ago.

With his upbeat attitude, insightful view about life and his longstanding interest and study of happiness, I was not a surprised when he told me he had begun teaching a personal development program at a local correctional facility or later when he began talks about the art of happiness at libraries and associations in the New York area. I was also delighted to find out he was writing a book on the same subject. Jim's natural understanding of the concept that "life is what you make it" along with his gift for teaching, was the perfect combination to launch a new career in motivational speaking.

As you read *Simple Happiness*, you will find that Jim's ideas are consistent with the aforementioned principles of positive psychology and positive reinforcement. He rightly points out that we need to have goals and dreams and then take small steps toward achieving them. Jim also recommends that we reward ourselves for partial successes along the way. He says that we can benefit from identifying things that are good for us and then focus on them. In other words, Jim's simple message is: find things that make you happy and then do more of those things.

Recent research has also shown that one of the best ways for people to be happy is by doing for others. It is interesting that happiness is not based on how much you achieve or how much material you own or accumulate. As Jim discusses, happy people give of themselves, which is consistent with that powerful concept.

Finally, Jim Ryan's passion and sincerity make him an excellent communicator and teacher. You will find that he presents his ideas in a very readable and understandable manner. *Enjoy!*

Introduction:
Opportunity Knocks

This book is not intended as a quick fix to change your life. It is meant for those who are looking for a little more out of life. To understand simple happiness is to realize that you have a choice in how you feel in any given time or situation. It is not a particular destination, but merely a state of awareness along your journey of life. You may already be on a quest for happiness. Or you may not. Perhaps you've never even given it a thought. No worries. You will still find something as you read that will lighten you up enough to recognize you are in the driver's seat.

Simple Happiness offers 52 easy ways to help you remove some of the mystery and confusion from your everyday life. Contrary to what some might say life does not have to be complicated and full of stress. Every day can be a new opportunity to experience joy.

You can certainly read through chapter after chapter, but it is not necessary. Each one represents a particular thought or idea to consider. They can stand alone or you'll find that some overlap in a similar concept. You might randomly read a chapter each day as a reminder to be in simple happiness. Or since there are 52 chapters, you might enjoy picking one per week for inspiration all year. As you read, you may find what I offer to be very basic, while others might find it quite profound. There are sections aimed to inspire you and others specifically meant to challenge you. Many offer practical steps or even spiritual solutions. No matter what, please be assured that everything I share in this book is meant for you!

Simple Happiness was written from the heart with the intent to give you comfort and hope. Comfort that no matter where you find yourself, it is just where you are supposed to be. All the experiences of your life have brought you to where you are now—in the right place at the right time. And it offers hope that no matter where that place is, it can always get better, much better. It represents comfort and hope that true happiness and joy are available to everyone—including you!

It is my further intent that these pages inspire you to look at the same old things in a brand new way. However this book finds you, it brings me joy to know that it may open doors for you that you didn't even know existed. I encourage you now to take the first step through a door of opportunity I like to call *Simple Happiness*. And as you do so, may you find what your heart desires.

The Basics

1

You Become What You Think About

Each of us has a powerful but untapped resource within us waiting to be discovered and utilized. We all have the potential of living a life with little or no stress—a life that is full of joy and fulfillment. This power lies in the ability to hang on to thoughts that empower us and let go of those thoughts that are disempowering to us. You become what you think about all day long.

Much has been written about this fundamental building block for explaining why some people always seem happy and why others rarely are. Mary Kay Ash said, "If you think you can, you can. And if you think you can't, you're right." For the most part, we decide what is going to happen before it happens. If you say to yourself, "I'll never be able to complete that 10k run," guess what? More than likely, you won't even begin to train. If you say to yourself, "Gee, look at all those people my age who are actually finishing that 10k run," you are more likely to give it a try. If you think you can, or think you can't, you're right!

Start to notice your thoughts throughout your day. Most of us think the same thoughts day after day. Most of our thoughts focus on "what is." It can be a real breakthrough just to be able to separate yourself from your thoughts. When you are able to step back and observe what thoughts you are hanging onto, you will start to understand why your life is the way it is.

Let's say you are thinking about your financial situation. You may be saying to yourself, "My parents always struggled to make ends meet." "I didn't have the educational opportunities that others had." "I guess I'm lucky to have my job, but I am still not able to get ahead." Your thoughts about "what is" in your life are going to get you more of "what is."

> *You become what you think about all day long.*

If you want things to change, you have to change something. Start by changing your thoughts. In his book, You'll See It When You Believe It, Wayne Dyer asserts that we can manifest what we want in our lives as long as we believe we can.

Take something in your life that you want to improve. Focus your thoughts on how you want things to be. As you focus on your desired result, notice how good you feel. Bring to mind your desired result and accompanying good feelings as often as you can during the day. Observe when the thought of the lack of your desired result enters your mind. Also notice the accompanying bad feelings. This is the exact moment to replace the thought of lack with the thought of fulfillment. Take charge! Make that thought of your desired result your dominant thought. Your life will start to move into the direction of your desires. Begin to fashion your own life. You become what you think about all day long.

2

Thought Systems

What is the nature of thought? Have you ever considered that? The answer is: "a thought is just a thought." That's it, nothing more, nothing less. Our thoughts do not necessarily have to become our reality. They become our reality when we focus on them or hang on to them until we make them our reality. If we could only hang on to the thoughts that empower us and let go of the ones that are disempowering to us, we'd all be a little happier. Did you ever wake up from a bad dream and, much to your relief, say to yourself, "Phew, it was just a dream"? If we could only say to ourselves about our thoughts as they pop into our heads, "Phew, it was just a thought!"

It sounds so simple. Let go of the thoughts that hurt us, hang on to the ones that help us. In practice, it's really not very easy. Why is it so difficult? It's difficult because we are who we are—creatures of our life experience. We may have already lived twenty, thirty, forty, fifty, sixty years or more. Over the years, we've learned to look at the world in our own unique way. We don't see the world as it truly is; we see the world as we are. We have developed our own way of processing and filtering everything that comes our way. Our thought systems have been formed by the people, experiences and situations that influence us along the way.

You have your thought systems, and I have mine. We seem to defend our thought systems as though our lives depended on them. These thought systems, which, over time, become our belief systems, can feel good or they can feel bad. Your job, if you want simple happiness, is to notice when you are hanging on to disempowering thoughts. When you observe yourself feeling sad, hurt, or depressed, you can usually trace that feeling back to how you were thinking about things. Observing yourself is the first step; choosing a better feeling thought is the next.

We are all creators of our own thoughts. Our emotions tell us whether our thoughts feel good or don't feel good. In our natural state of mind, our thoughts flow freely and easily. When we are stuck in our ego, which is driven by outside influences, we activate thoughts that can ultimately be disempowering to us. We can dwell on the negative emotion that arises or we can use it as a signal to reach for a more empowering thought.

When you understand that your thought systems

work alongside your emotional body, you can take control of how you want to feel in any given situation. You begin to realize that recasting your thought systems is a major breakthrough in your search for simple happiness.

3

Your Natural State of Mind

In order to make changes in your life, you must start by looking at things differently. Your old views, your old ways of thinking, could be the reason that you are not as happy as you might be. Your old thought systems keep repeating the same way to deal with circumstances in the same manner time after time, the same way you always have. But how do you begin to change your perspective when you don't see it any other way?

What if you explored the possibility that there might be another way to look at things? What if you could bring a perspective to situations that would not cause you to be upset, saddened or disturbed? What if you could bring an outlook to a situation that would leave you feeling peaceful and confident? This other view sits quietly beside our thought systems, waiting for to you tap into it. It is known as our natural state of mind; a place where there is peace, solutions to problems, creativity and a general feeling of personal well-being!

How do we get from our thought systems to our

natural state of mind? The first step is that you have to want to be there. Some of us wouldn't trade our thought systems for anything. Some think there is only one way to look at things and that's their way! For those of us looking for a more peaceful, less stressful life, we can find it in our natural state of mind.

We have all experienced our natural state of mind when we take a break from our thought systems. Suppose you have plans to pick your friend up for a day of shopping, but you can't find your keys. You look here, there, and everywhere! Frustrated, you call your friend and have to reschedule your shopping trip. You gradually calm down as you go on to another activity at home. After awhile, guess what happens—you remember where your keys are! You knew all along, but in your frustration, their whereabouts eluded you. When you stopped fretting, the answer appeared effortlessly. That's your natural state of mind at work. All the answers, solutions and inspirations are always available to us. Sometimes our thought systems get in the way and keep them from surfacing to our consciousness.

So you want to get to your natural state of mind. Now what? Next, we have to practice the experience of being there. Here's one way to do it. Turn off the TV, the stereo, the phone, and anything else that might distract you. Sit quietly in a comfortable chair and relax. Keep your focus on your breathing—you breathe in, you breathe out. Continue to breathe in and out quietly.

A thought will come to mind. You recognize it as a thought and you let it pass out of your head, again focusing on your breathing. What is this exercise called? That's right, meditation!

This practice of quieting your brain allows you to access the power of your natural state of mind. The more you experience your natural state of mind through meditation, the better equipped you will be to access that state when you want to. The trick is to notice when your thought systems are causing you to feel bad. When you notice a bad feeling, instead of reacting in a way that can make the situation worse, you will be able to access your natural state of mind and deal with the situation from a different perspective. Moving to your natural state of mind gives you a chance to deal with the situation from a position of patience and compassion, which in turn will offer an outcome that will most likely be much more satisfying to you.

There are many fine books you can read about meditation. In its essence, meditation is nothing more than quieting the mind and letting thoughts go from your head. You'll get better at it with daily practice. The more you practice the easier it will be to gain access to your natural state of mind.

This ready access comes in handy also when you begin to feel stress. As you begin to feel the first signs of stress, take notice. It is in noticing the stress that helps you to slow down. In this slower state you understand that the thoughts causing the stress are just thoughts. Once you realize that they are just thoughts, you can more easily move into your natural state of mind, deal more peacefully with them, and then let them go. Practicing being in your natural state of mind is a fun way to discover that simple happiness is not even a thought away!

4

From Point A to Point B

It is not easy to make wholesale changes in our lives. Crash diets rarely work long term. We take off weight quickly by drastically changing our food intake in some way. It works great for a while, but eventually we fall off the wagon and gain back the weight we lost and then some. The best way to long-term weight control is to alter our diet in small bites. Gaining control of what we eat in a gradual way so we don't feel deprived and resent the process. The same is true for all life-altering changes as well.

When it comes to changing our thinking so we can live in simple happiness, the same principal applies. Our goal everyday can be to go from point A, (where we currently are), to point B, (a small improvement over point A).

Maybe your goal for the day is to be more appreciative of the good things that are happening in your life rather than taking them for granted. Take notice of your thoughts as you consciously give thanks for your ability to see, hear or speak. This small step, and its associated good feelings, may motivate you to be more appreciative that day.

Maybe the next day your goal is to be compassionate towards others. That thought will help you focus on being kind to those you meet. Notice the good feelings that accompany your effort to be compassionate. Each evening as you spend some quite time reflecting, you can do a quick mental review of the day's efforts. You can then set a small performance goal in your mind for the next day.

It is in the daily awareness of making small positive steps that strong, permanent changes occur. It is in noticing also the good feelings that accompany these small steps that motivates us to do more. Your conscious progress towards happiness becomes a daily focus in your life. Having gone from point A to point B today may even give you the feeling of excitement over what may be in store for you as you wake up tomorrow to begin a new point A in hopes of reaching another point B.

5

Why You Need Teachers

From our first days of life through our early twenties, our personal development is monitored very closely. All the way through our final years in high school, we are guided and graded by our parents, family members, teachers, coaches, ministers, doctors and whoever else is there to see us through childhood.

As we become young adults and mandatory education has been completed, we are faced with significant choices: going to college, getting a job, or joining the military. Now life becomes a bit more serious and success is placed directly on our own shoulders. From this point, we begin to make our own choices, which are not always easy or triumphant. Some flunk out of college. Some are asked to leave the military. Some get fired from jobs. While there are many who move toward positive life paths, there are those who find that continued growth and personal development grinds to a halt. Now faced with life head on, they begin to falter. Some figure they have all the answers. Others leave tremendous potential unfulfilled.

As adults, we are always running into forks in the road. One leads toward growth and development, the other leads to more of the same. For many of us, more of the same is the easier, more comfortable path to take. We choose more of the same because we tell ourselves, "That's who I am. That's how I've always done it!" The road to progress sometimes feels lonely and frightening. The fear of where the road may take us can be paralyzing. Unfortunately, by avoiding the risks, we sometimes never get to experience the rewards that await us.

> *...everyone who comes into your life does so to teach you a lesson.*

The key to navigating the road to self-growth is to seek out teachers who can show us the way. Often it seems that certain people are self-made achievers. But if you speak to successful people, most will tell you that they had some help along the way—people who motivated them. Teachers in adulthood are like teachers in childhood. They challenge us. They encourage us. They correct us. They open doors to innovative ideas within us. They inspire us to be and do more.

Where do we find such teachers in the adult world? It could be where we found them before—in school (college, trade school), at home or at church. But often, we find them in unexpected places. A teacher might be your boss or co-worker, a friend, your spouse or children, or even your grandchildren. We find teachers in the media—TV, radio, movies, tapes, CDs and books. Teachers even show up as strangers or people we meet who may only briefly cross our paths. Ultimately, everyone who comes into your life does so to teach you a lesson.

For us to grow as adults, we must begin with the desire or intention to do so. We must say to ourselves, "I don't want to be the same person next year that I am today. I want to be a better person." We must seek out fresh ways of thinking since new ideas are the lifeblood of personal growth.

As you pursue your dreams and open yourself to the guidance available to you, the appropriate teachers will show up who can aid in your discovery of life-changing ideas!

6

When the Student is Ready, the Teacher Will Appear

You can't catch a baseball until you can keep your mitt on your hand. You can't hit a ball until you can hold the bat. You can't go to third base until you've touched second base. There is a certain readiness that is required for us to learn certain things.

This is especially true of our adult development. Psychologist Carl Jung taught that there are four stages of adulthood: the Athlete, the Warrior, the Statesman and the Spiritual Person. In the first stage, our physical prowess determines our worth; i.e. our athletic ability, our good looks. In the Warrior stage, we realize that to make it in the business world, we must have more than good looks. Here we realize the need to develop other skills, which will help us succeed. The Statesman is one who has achieved a certain status and decides to give back to his community in some form or another. Finally, the Spiritual person realizes that there is more to life than what we can experience through our senses.

He cultivates his divine side and in so doing, lives a fuller, more joyful life.

We are all on a path to somewhere. Each of us are going and growing at our own speed. As we advance through Jung's four stages of adulthood, certainly we will receive assistance from various sources along the way.

I'm sure that as you look over your life, there have been people (teachers) who have aided your growth and development. The Buddhist saying, "When the student is ready, the teacher will appear," comes into play as we become more conscious of that path on which we travel. It could be a person you just met or a seminar you attended or even a book you are reading. Sometimes when you least expect it, you will realize that you have experienced something new; something exciting that has changed you. You experience an instant awakening. Something that confounded you previously now becomes clear. You shake your head and say, "Wow!"

These incredible turns in consciousness come at just the right moment. It happens because you are now ready to experience it. As you move along your life path, be aware that everything you experience gets you ready for the next teacher to appear. Each opportunity for growth prepares you to more deeply appreciate what comes next. You not only begin to recognize a teacher, but seek them out for guidance. Though some unfortunately never get to this point of understanding, many are happily realizing that they always have support. By grasping the notion of being in the right place at the right time, your journey becomes easier, more direct and extraordinarily rewarding.

Things to Think About

$$\underset{\displaystyle 7}{\overset{\displaystyle \diagdown\!\diagup\!\diagdown}{}}$$

You Live in a Mansion

Have you ever been in a mansion? Maybe it was one of the fabulous Newport, Rhode Island mansions. Or perhaps it was a stately southern plantation. You might have gone on a local house tour to view a beautiful home. Did you feel the excitement as you approached the front door with the prospect of exploring the entire home, experiencing the drama of each room that you visited?

You passed through the imposing front door and gasped as you took in the large entrance foyer. You admired everything: the chandelier, the crown moldings, the wall coverings, the finish on the floors, and the grandfather clock; everything!

The foyer was indeed impressive, but would you have been satisfied totally, just seeing the first room? Would you have been ready to say to your friend who was visiting the mansion with you, "You go ahead and tour the rest of the rooms; I'm going to stay here. This is enough for me!" I hardly think so! Seeing the foyer would be just enough to whet your appetite for more. Most likely, you would have great anticipation to see the other rooms: the front parlor, the back parlor, the dining room, the library, the kitchen, the butler's pantry and the winding staircase to visit the bedrooms upstairs.

What excitement as you step into each room, beautifully decorated, each with its own charm; its own character, its own story to tell. How satisfying it is, upon finishing the tour, to discuss your favorite parts with your friend and to appreciate the mansion all over again.

You see, your life is like a mansion. Each of us has the potential to live a life of complete joy and fulfillment. The problem is that we spend most, if not all, of our lives living in the foyer. It is a life of experiencing the same things over and over again—a life of little growth or fulfillment.

I challenge you to explore the other rooms in your mansion. One room may contain food for the cultivation of your mind through inspiring books. A second room might be the experience of unconditional love, perhaps for your family, loving without asking anything in return. A third might be giving 100% at work instead of just sliding by, doing as little as possible. A fourth might be developing the habit of only saying good things about others, whether they are present or not. Another might be expanding your spiritual side through daily meditation. A sixth might be developing your talents- through music, athletics, art or whatever they may be. A seventh might be doing some volunteer work for the good of your fellow man-giving of yourself in service so that someone else's life could be better.

Take a look at yourself. Are you living your life in the foyer of your mansion? It might seem easy and feel comfortable to just stay in the foyer, but why not try opening up some doors and peeking in? Your mansion may contain even more incredible rooms that I have failed to mention. My promise to you is that once you start to venture into the other rooms of your own personal mansion, your life will forever be changed for the better!

8

What is Compassion?

Have a little compassion. We've all heard that expression. But what does it really mean? When I ask that question at my presentations, I get answers that you would expect: empathy, feelings for others, kindness and understanding. Though these answers are all correct, let me tell you what compassion means to me.

One evening when I was giving a talk in my local library, I was telling a story about a woman on my block who would never acknowledge me when our paths crossed. I would always give a friendly wave hello as I passed her during my walks or if she came by my house as I was doing yard work. Each time she would look away or put her head down, averting her eyes from mine. I couldn't understand why in the world this woman always ignored my friendly hellos. After all, I was being friendly. "What is the matter with her?" I asked, sounding somewhat annoyed. And then a woman in the second row raised her hand and quietly offered, "Maybe she is shy."

It was at that moment that I got a lesson in the real meaning of compassion! Here I was, giving a talk on happiness and exhibiting a total lack of compassion. Sure I was being friendly to my neighbor, but I also was holding an expectation in that friendliness. That evening, I learned that compassion is allowing others to be who they want to be. Compassion is not expecting or demanding that others be who we want them to be. Compassion is not judging the actions of others according to our standards and values. Compassion is cutting others some slack instead of criticizing them. Compassion is not a feeling of superiority. It is the realization and acknowledgement of the dignity that each one of us possesses as a human being. It is a basic understanding that every one of us is doing his best to figure things out. We are all on our own path through life. Compassion is the conscious decision to send out love to all those who cross our path.

What a load off the shoulders! We don't have to get upset when people do things differently than the way we would like them to. It is extremely liberating to allow others to be who they are. When we are compassionate to others, we bring simple happiness to ourselves.

Are We Really Creatures of Habit?

I'm sure you've heard the expression, "You are a creature of habit." Maybe you've said it yourself. Another common phrase is, "That's the way I've always done it!"

What makes us do the things we do? Why do we react to situations the way we do? Sometimes we use the excuses listed above. Sometimes we try to pin our reactions on our heredity or on our environment: that age old paradigm.

My contention is that all these ideas are merely excuses that we use to defend our mediocrity and shortcomings. Certainly, we have a genetic make-up. We were brought up with certain value systems. It seems that these value systems make us think we can't change. It is our tendency to react to situations the way we have reacted in the past.

Let me suggest to you that there is another way to look at this. We experience a circumstance (a stimulus) and we react to that circumstance either in thought or deed (a response). Our life is a series of stimuli and responses. Often there is no thought at all given to the situation. There is no gap between the stimulus and the response. Something happens and we react. Often we react the way we always have because we are creatures of habit. We give absolutely no thought whatsoever to our response. We just react.

As with so many things in life, there is another way of doing things, another way to look at things. We can, if we intend to do so, notice the stimulus as it happens. As we notice the stimulus happening, a small gap occurs. That gap allows a space for us to react differently from the way we always have reacted. That small gap gives us a chance to consider our choices in dealing with the stimulus. We can consider how we want to react to that circumstance. Our response can now come from a place of heightened consciousness, not experienced when we simply react as creatures of habit. We may still offer the same response we have in the past, but now we realize that it is a conscious choice, rather than an uncontrolled act. As we deal with the feelings that result from our chosen response, we have the opportunity to notice how we feel. We then have another choice to make. Am I happy with the way I responded? Or could I have handled the situation better and felt better about myself? That consciousness is an awareness of what is happening as it happens. Some would say it is living in the moment. This consciousness gives us the opportunity to choose a response.

Developing this consciousness requires the intention to do so. It does require practice. That practice involves the effort to notice ourselves as we respond to stimulus after stimulus throughout our day.

You can choose peace in your responses. You can choose to be kind. You can choose to be compassionate. The point is: you get to choose. You are a creature of habit either because you want to be or because you don't know any better. Now you know better!

10

It's a Long Life

"It's a long life." There are two basic ways of looking at that statement. One, life seems like it's getting longer and longer. Technology, nutrition and medical science continue to advance, pushing the average life span further out. It seems like a tough road to make it all the way. Or two, we have plenty of time to embark on as many journeys as it takes to live the life of our dreams. We have many chances to start over, new opportunities to reset our goals and more possibilities to change our legacy.

You may believe that you had a lousy childhood. As you become a parent you have the chance to be the parent you thought you should have had. Maybe you feel bad about the way you raised your kids. Now that your children are grown, you can make up for lost time by offering loving support in their choices as adults and when they become parents. Grandparenting is another chance to love unconditionally. Another opportunity to start over is after the kids are grown and out of the house. You can reconnect with your spouse with a new sense of appreciation.

If you feel that life is passing you by, then it probably is! You can fret about lost opportunities, chastising yourself for living a life of little consequence. You could live each day going through the motions in a joyless fashion, thinking up excuses for why your life has turned out the way it has or you can listen to the wake up call! Jump aboard "the passing life" and start living it! Make choices that move you into the direction of a more fulfilling life. You don't need to wait for a milestone event such as a birth, a marriage, or even a death, to get you thinking about your legacy. Start thinking about it now! Someone once said, "The definition of old age is when regrets take the place of dreams"!

> *Shine the light on others as you age and you will see the joy of living a long life.*

Let's say you've reached a ripe old age. Now what? Challenges may arise as you lose the ability to do the things you used to do when you were young. It takes a lot of humility to age gracefully. Don't fall into the trap of getting discouraged and disheartened by the aging process. The true opportunity of "the golden years" is that it can be a time of enlightenment, appreciation, and graceful being.

As you reach this stage in life, develop some new strategies for maintaining a positive outlook. The same principles of happiness exist in old age as they did in your younger, more vigorous days. Live by the "golden rule" and don't take yourself so seriously. True growth comes in seeking out opportunities to brighten up the lives of others even as your own light fades. Rise above the challenges of aging by deflecting your conversations away from complaints. Wisdom lies more in listening to and supporting those around you than any words you might say.

Shine the light on others as you age and you will see the joy of living a long life.

Are You a Human Doing or Human Being?

"Are we human doings or human beings?" This is a question raised by author, lecturer and spiritual guru, Dr. Deepak Chopra. From the minute we open our eyes each day, we're on the go. Things to do, people to see, places to go. Listening to the news as we shave, putting on make-up while driving to work, eating lunch at a staff meeting, on our cell phone at the Little League game. Being busy validates our existence. Multi-tasking seems to be the modern day philosophy. We can't wait to finish one thing so we can start the next.

One day runs into the next, one week runs into another. Before you know it, another year has passed. Where does the time go? Don't get me wrong. I'm in favor of achievement and living life to its fullest potential. But there is more to living than being busy. By becoming aware of your natural state of being, as described in meditation, you can bring that experience into your everyday activities.

It is in the "being" not just the "doing" that you can reveal your true self that hides beneath the doing. You can experience your genius self, your loving self, your appreciating self, your wonderful self who doesn't always have to take himself so seriously. You may even stop identifying yourself by what you earn, where you live, what you do, and what you have.

Part of this "being" idea is to stay in touch with who you are while "doing." This conscious awareness of who you really are can lend another dimension to everything you do. Instead of being swallowed up by the stresses of life, your sense of being can bring a calming perspective. Instead of feeling overwhelmed, your sense of being can help you maintain balance. Even your enjoyable experiences, such as watching a spectacular sunset or working in the garden can be enhanced.

As a human "being," you can see yourself not as a mundane "do-er" in life, but as a pure child of God, here to experience the wonderful connection to our Source.

12

Being Prepared is Half the Battle

What do coaches in the National Football League do the first thing on Monday morning after a Sunday game? They start watching film of the game played the day before. Then they preview footage of the team they will play on the following Sunday. Throughout the week, they practice on situations they might encounter in their next game. They study the opposing team so they can negate their strengths and exploit their weaknesses. And when Sunday comes, they are fully prepared for their opponent.

My first career was as a foreign language teacher in a Junior High School. The material for teaching first year French was basic so it allowed me to focus more on my students. Almost all of my preparation was in anticipation of challenges students might bring to class. In this way, I was prepared to deal with them in a constructive way. My classroom goal was for my students to learn to speak French and enjoy themselves in the process. My strategy was to head off any problems before they distracted the class. If a student did not complete his homework, I was ready to help him. I would catch a disruptive student in the hall, letting her know that I expected excellent participation that day. My attempt was to create the best learning atmosphere possible. By preparing myself in advance, I was able to proactively offer positive solutions to situations as they arose instead of a negative reaction that was less than constructive. As a result, most students enjoyed my class and my career in teaching was one of the most rewarding experiences of my life.

Consider your daily life. Where are the situations that pose difficulty? Being prepared begins with four easy steps:

1. Notice where improvement may be needed.
2. Have the intention to make progress.
3. Develop a constructive strategy for dealing with the situation.
4. Rehearse your strategy in your mind before the event occurs. How will you react? What will you say? Will you yell? Will you listen? Will you hug? Will you express your love?

Another part of being prepared is to spend time daily in meditation. You don't necessarily need to be thinking about any specific problem area. Once you give your intent on preparing yourself for certain situations, your mind is ready to search for answers. As you relax and just be, you'll be amazed at the great ideas that reveal themselves to you. Creative solutions will become evident. Some of our best answers come when we take the time to stop trying to figure things out. It's all part of being prepared.

13

Moods are not Terminal

Have you ever noticed that your moods are like a rollercoaster that is constantly going up and down? First you're in a good mood and then suddenly you are in a low mood. If you are ever going to live in simple happiness, it's important to understand your moods.

The first important thing to recognize is that moods don't last forever. They come and go, while your life stays pretty much the same. Observe: when you're in a good mood, almost nothing bothers you. When you are in a low mood, anything can bother you. It's not that your life circumstance suddenly changes; it's only your mood that changes!

The problem is that when you're in a low mood, everything gets serious. That's when you want to get to the bottom of things. That's when you have to get things off your chest. You often find yourself going on the attack. It's almost as if you have drawn both guns from their holsters and you begin firing the barrels toward everything and everyone in your life—pow, pow, pow!

You might say, "You can't talk to me that way!" or "I'm sick and tired of the way you've been treating me!" or "I can't stand this or that!"

Now let's say you're attacking your spouse in this manner. She will most likely react in one of two ways. She will quickly pull down an invisible shield between you, forcing your bullets to ricochet right back at you. Her eyes will glaze over, her ears will lock shut and she won't listen to a word that you say. You then become even more infuriated because you get no reaction. Or, she may collect herself, take a stand, draw both of her pistols from their holsters and fire back at you with her guns blazing. And depending upon what's been building up in her, you might find yourself staring down much larger barrels!

Have you ever solved any problems this way? I doubt it! Usually the opposite will occur. Hurtful things may be said that make the original situation even worse. Trying to solve problems when in a low mood is like trying to watch TV when the cable is out. You can't do it. You have to wait until the cable is restored before you can enjoy your show.

If you have the intention to grow in this area, there are a few things to consider. To begin with, it helps to know when you are in a low mood. As with most situations, a conscious awareness of what is going on in your head is critical. Notice if you feel the urge to take everything very seriously. That's the time to back off, to keep your mouth shut. Remember, it's not your life that has changed—just your mood! Try to engage in a quite activity; listen to music, take a walk, read a magazine. This will help switch your thoughts to lighter things. But most of all, do not engage in any serious discussion at that time.

Once you recognize that your low mood has passed, (as it always does), that's when you can reconsider the situation. When you are in a better mood, think back to what was so important. If it still is an issue that you feel you need to discuss, (and it may not be), you'll be much better equipped to arrive at a solution when approaching it in a loving, caring way, instead of with guns blazing. Remember, these same concepts apply if you are on the receiving end of those blazing guns!

Your moods are not necessarily terminal, but your actions based on them can be. As you become more deliberate in choosing your state of being, your conscious awareness grows and your life naturally becomes more relaxed and in control.

14

You've Raised Your Kids, Now All You Have to Do is Love Them

If you're a parent, raising your kids is certainly one of the most important things you'll ever do in life. Each couple or single parent finds their own way. Some are strict, some are lenient, some yell and some admonish calmly. Raising kids is a very personal undertaking. Sometimes it is very easy to criticize the methods of other parents. But, surprisingly, most kids turn out just fine, despite the judgment of others.

One basic premise of raising kids is that they learn much more by our actions than by our words. In raising our kids, we are giving them a legacy. Luck has very little to do with it. Kids learn more by what they see than by the words we dictate.

Part of raising kids is teaching them to be independent, decision-making adults. Some do a better job at it than others. Regardless, as children become adults, the role of the parent changes. It becomes one of love and support rather than the continued hands-on nurturing of the earlier years.

Most young adults feel good about spreading their wings, leaving the nest and making a life of their own. That's your opportunity as a parent to let them live it as they choose. Think back to when you were younger. Did you like being told about a better way of doing things or did you like figuring things out on your own? Telling your child that you respect his or her choices can go a long way. Keeping the lines of communication open is crucial. Some parents encourage their children to come to them for advice. Although it is a step in the right direction, remember that unconditional love should always be the underlining message.

> *...unconditional love should always be the underlining message.*

Things can become even more wonderful when your children marry and have their own children. Bang! Just like that, your family grows. Your love and support can now bring more joy than you ever expected.

Sometimes when grandchildren come along, the stress levels begin to rise because the younger generation is doing things differently than you did. This is when you have a choice: to press your views or to simply allow your adult children to parent as they see fit. When confronted with a situation that you disapprove of, focus on being a loving support instead of being critical.

And the circle of life continues to go around. New generations are born. Roles change. Tell your kids how proud you are of them. Love them more than ever and leave it at that!

15

That's All the Lumber You Sent

I was in the music department of a bookstore a couple of years ago to pick up a copy of James Taylor's latest CD. After my purchase, I went to the new release section where they let you listen to CDs before buying them. Here I found a CD by Kathy Mattea and listened to the first song.

It was about a man who had recently passed away. St. Peter met the man at the gates of Heaven and asked him if he would like to see the house they had built for him, where he was to live for all of eternity. The man anxiously agreed.

They began to walk down a beautiful wide boulevard with tremendous stone mansions on either side, each one beautifully landscaped. The man was now starting to get excited. As they strolled down the boulevard, the houses became a little more modest and the road a bit less wide. The homes were fabulous nonetheless.

As they walked and walked, the homes got smaller and smaller. The street got narrower and narrower.

Finally at the end of a dirt road, St. Peter stopped and pointed to a tiny shack, barely livable. He said to the man "Well, here it is."

The man couldn't believe it. He said to St. Peter, "You mean this is the home you've prepared for me to live in for all eternity? You've got to be kidding! How can you do this to me?" St. Peter humbly said to the man. "That's all the lumber you sent."

The song goes on to say that those living in the mansions found out early what it's all about: love and compassion for your fellow man. The recently deceased man wants to go back to earth and do it again. He professes to St. Peter the kind of life he would lead in order to send an abundance of lumber to construct his heavenly home.

I am always somewhat saddened when I hear of a person who, having survived some tragic event, (perhaps cancer or a heart attack), decides to change his life and find a way to live a life of purpose. It's not the person's decision to change his life that saddens me, but the fact that a tragedy had to occur to break the person out of his inertia.

Break out now! Start sending more lumber. Live a purposeful life, filled with unconditional love and compassion.

16

Stress is a Choice

One of the recurring themes in this book is that our life is a series of choices. In my Simple Happiness talk, I examine how happy people have the intention to be happy. They realize that it is not luck or fortunate circumstances that bring them happiness in the long run. Happy people also know that bad luck and unfortunate circumstances do not bring them misery in the long run. Happy people understand that it is the way we deal with the circumstances that makes all the difference. Everyday we come face to face with situations that elicit a reaction from us. It is in how we choose to react from moment to moment, that we fashion our lives.

Let's discuss stress. It's an epidemic causing countless diseases. For many, stress is seen as an uncontrollable response to the pressures of society today. Some will say, "I have no choice" when confronted with challenges, then they choose stress as their reaction. Stress is a choice.

The key to avoiding stress is to first become aware

of what makes you feel stressed. I find most of the stress in my life results from the following:

1. Taking myself too seriously.
2. Expecting others to act the way I think they should act.
3. Being concerned about what others think of me.

If you really want to lower stress in your life, then you absolutely must recognize it as it is happening. Once you are able to step back from the "stressful circumstance", you will begin to see that you have choices.

Let's say you were attempting to merge onto the highway and the driver next to you sped up and would not let you merge in front of him. As a result, you had to hit the brakes and quickly slip in behind him to avoid an accident as the merging lane quickly came to an end. You felt that the driver next to you should have seen your directional signal and let you merge in front of him. But he didn't! You are faced with a choice on how you react. You could say to yourself:

A.   "How dare that guy speed up and not let me merge onto the parkway ahead of him. I had my directional signal on. He made me have to slam on my brakes and almost cause an accident. That really ticks me off! I should speed up, pass him and then cut in front of him. See how he likes having to slam on his brakes. I'll show him!"

Or

B.   "Hey, that guy could have let me in. Alright,

I guess I should have let him go first anyway. He did have the right of way. Thank God I hit the breaks in time to avoid hitting that other car. Okay, it's over. Let it go. This is not worth getting upset about."

By noticing that you felt anger in the moment that your were feeling it gives you the opportunity to look at the situation more objectively so that you can choose how to react. It is always your call. You can choose stress by getting angry or you can choose to feel good by relaxing, letting go, and finding a positive thought or phrase. A friend of mine says to his wife in similar situations, "What do you care?" Why not say that or come up with an expression of your own that diffuses your stress when it occurs? You can embrace the stress or let it go. It's your choice!

Some people have a hard time stepping back because they don't want to step back. Their identity is tied to their stress. They look for it. They love it. They spend their energy looking to be offended. When they start a sentence, "You'll never believe what happened to me today," you can be sure that what is to follow is going to be negative. These people are choosing stress.

When you notice yourself getting upset over how another person is acting, you again have a choice to make. Do you make a critical judgment about the person and be annoyed? Do you then go around telling everyone you meet that day how annoyed you were by that person? Or do you recognize that you have another choice on how to react? You could bring to mind a compassionate thought and send out love to that person. You can consciously give that person permission to do things the way he wants to do things. You have the choice to say to yourself, "It's ok! He doesn't need to do things exactly the way I would." Allowing others to be who they are without letting it affect you in a negative way is liberating. A tremendous weight can be lifted off your shoulders just by making the simple choice of compassion over judgment.

One final thought about choices, which says it best, comes from a poem by Mother Theresa of Calcutta.

THE FINAL ANALYSIS

People are often unreasonable, illogical and self-centered. Forgive them anyway.

If you are kind, people may accuse you of selfish, ulterior motives. Be kind anyway.

If you are successful, you will win some false friends and some true enemies. Succeed anyway.

If you are honest and frank, people may cheat you. Be honest and frank anyway.

What you spend years building, someone may destroy overnight. Build anyway.

If you find serenity and happiness, they may be jealous. Be happy anyway.

The good you do today, people will often forget tomorrow. Do good anyway.

Give the world the best you have, and it may never be enough. Give the world the best you have anyway.

You see, in the final analysis, it is all between you and God. It was never between you and them anyway.

— Mother Theresa of Calcutta

In the Middle of the Difficulty Lies Opportunity

How we look at things makes all the difference in the world. Albert Einstein said, "In the middle of the difficulty lies opportunity." How we deal with the challenges in our lives all depends upon the way we choose to see the situation. Along the same train of thought, Wayne Dyer says, "If you change the way you look at things, the things you look at change."

Imagine how great your life would be if you had no problems, nothing to feel stressed about. I think that kind of life is worth pursuing. However, in order to move in the right direction, we must take the necessary steps. Most of us don't enjoy our troubles. We may even wish that they didn't exist and hope that they would magically go away. But in thinking about our problems, we only make things worse. Dwelling on what ails us only causes continued stress and anxiety. We often discuss our difficulties with others more in an attempt to get sympathy, rather than true resolution. Let's

JIM RYAN

consider two basic tenets of this book: "Our lives become what we think about all day long" and "The only person you can change is you!"

What if, instead of looking at the difficulties in your life as problems, you took a turn in your consciousness to see them as opportunities? The whole notion of an opportunity would be the complete opposite from that of a problem. Everything would change. You would go from associating problems with stress, anxiety and worry, to correlating the good feelings that come along with opportunities. From a defensive, powerless state, you instantly see all the possibilities and your creative mind expands. Problems disappear because solutions would always be evident. All of a sudden, what once brought you stress and anxiety now brings you excitement and enthusiasm. What a joy life would be! No more problems—just opportunities!

By changing the way you look at people, the people you look at change.

Okay, so it's not so easy to make that kind of turn in consciousness. Like the proverbial "old dog trying to learn a new trick", you would need to first practice changing the way you look at things. It takes clear intent and willingness to allow a new way of thinking to make its way into your consciousness. Sometimes your old way of thinking is what causes problems.

You will need to get out of your own way. The best approach to learning is by experience. It is at the precise point of difficulty that the opportunity is staring you in the face. The decision to change your view in that moment will be the catalyst for making the shift in your outlook down the line. Victor Frankl stated it so clearly, "When we are no longer able to change a situation, we are challenged to change ourselves." Once mastered, opportunities will fill your life.

For example, if you find that a co-worker constantly aggravates you, perhaps it is time to see her in a whole new light. In considering the Buddhist saying, "Everyone who comes into my life does so to teach me a lesson," you can start to appreciate her placement in your life. Instead of regarding her annoyances as a problem and all the negatives mindsets that go along with that problem, you could look at her as being there to teach you a lesson. In this case, we could take the word "things" in Dyer's quote and substitute the word "people." By changing the way you look at *people*, the *people* you look at change.

"In the middle of the difficulty lies opportunity." By looking at disconcerting people or stressful circumstances from this new perspective, the lessons will jump right out to teach you. Perhaps you are to learn about patience, compassion, cooperation or even forgiveness. Regardless of the challenges that come your way—and they will, remember they are only opportunities for you to grow.

It's All Made Up Anyway

An auto accident occurs at a busy intersection in the city. Upon investigation, the police find out that there were four eyewitnesses. The police interview each witness in order to determine the details of the accident. Every eyewitness gives a slightly different account of what they witnessed. It seems ridiculous, but it's true. It happens all the time. We experience the same circumstance as others, but we see things very differently. Which story is real?

There is a story of two sneaker companies that each sends a marketing representative to a small African country to assess the prospects of business expansion. One representative sends back an e-mail saying, "It's a dead end; everyone is barefoot." The other representative sends back his e-mail saying, "The sky is the limit; everyone is barefoot!"

What's important to recognize is that we all create our lives by they way we see things. You are literally making it up as you go along! What is real to one person is unreal to another. Some people tend to see the good side of things and some people tend to see the bad. You may have heard someone say, "Oh no, I'm not a pessimist; I'm a realist!" We all tend to defend the way we are or how we see things. Are you someone who takes an optimistic or pessimistic perspective? You always have a choice. How do you want the story of your life to be?

Pay attention to your general attitude. Are you irritable most the time or are you good-natured? Start to notice what thoughts you are hanging on to throughout your day. Are they thoughts that are hopeful or cynical? Do you wonder if your commute to work is going to be a colossal pain or do you anticipate an opportunity to relax and enjoy your book on tape? Do you tell yourself that you're going to have a great time at a party or do you anxiously expect to have a lousy time? If you tend to be one who sees the glass as half empty, try telling yourself that the party will be great. See what happens. The reality is that you are the one who decides. And if it is all made up anyway, why not make up something that is good for you?

Realizing that we are the ones who fashion our lives by how we choose to respond to the circumstances of our lives might just be the turning point towards a happier, more joyful life. Free yourself from your old, limiting attitudes. Embrace the exhilarating freedom that is yours as you shed your negativity for something better, much better. Why not? It's all made up anyway!

Take a Look at Yourself

What Makes You Happy?

Author Rita Mae Brown put it very well when she wrote, "I finally figured it out. The only reason to be alive is to enjoy it." In my talks, I often ask the audience, "Who has an activity that they love to do, an activity that makes time fly by unnoticed?" I point out that it can be an activity that melts stress away or it can be an activity that puts them in a state of flow, a state of joy. The responses from the audience are amazingly varied: reading, gardening, listening to music, painting, writing, playing golf, working out, walking, and so forth. It is easy to see those who are sincere in their passions by how quickly they raise their hands and the enthusiasm in their voices as they share! What a blessing it is to have something that you love to do, something that brings you joy and satisfaction.

What I find of equal interest is that many people don't know how to answer that question. It's as if they don't have an activity that fills them with passion. It happens with every group—some respond right away, while others sit quietly and say nothing. It could very well be that they have something they love to do, but simply choose not to share it. But it is a sad thought to think that a person might not identify with any activity that brings them true joy.

Take a look at yourself. Are you having fun during your day? Do you have something that you look forward to doing? If you don't, there are plenty of opportunities out there for you. Take a look at your adult education bulletin. Is there a class that piques your interest? What about your local library? Stop in and ask about their programs and activities. Local libraries have become community centers offering many interesting activities. Churches, too, offer many opportunities to get involved, both in service to others and socially.

Don't forget, there are two parts to this equation. The first is in knowing what brings you joy. The second is finding time to pursue your interest. Many of us find ourselves in a situation that does not seem to offer the time for such fun. We have highly committed family responsibilities or demanding work schedules. Perhaps it's a long commute to work that takes up our mornings and evenings. The tendency for most is to put things off to a later date when we think will have more time or perhaps enough money. Certainly, these circumstances can be real. But if we allow them to get in the way of what we enjoy, they may become the cause of resentment. And that will only keep you further from not only finding what makes you happy, but doing it.

Know what makes you happy and find time to do it! Developing your talents is one of life's greatest sources of satisfaction. Sometimes just a little time away helps you come back refreshed and better equipped to handle whatever life may bring your way. Making time for you is not a selfish attitude, but a self-loving one. Often, all that is needed is a small compromise with your spouse or your boss- an effort that is well worth making.

If you are not already doing what makes you happy, then now is as good a time as any to begin. Letting your light shine not only brightens up your own life, but inspires those around you to brighten up their lives as well!

20

Are Your Antennas Up?

Our lives are full of choices. Once we realize this, everything can start to change. Start to observe your thoughts and actions. Observe the choices you make, observe your reactions to circumstances that confront you as you go through your day.

Do you put your blinders on every morning? You know, those eye shields that help horses keep their eyes straight ahead so that they can't look to the left or to the right. Is your daily goal to just get through the day, not causing anyone any problems? Do you just do what you have to do so that you can get home, eat, slip into your jammies and curl up in front of the T.V. for the evening? You know the routine. Get up, go to work, and come home—day after day. That's what many of us do. It's our choice.

On the other hand, are you a person who starts their day and chooses to put up your antennas? Do you wonder to yourself, "What good will come my way today?" Do you think to yourself, "I wonder whose life I can make a little better today?" When you have your antennas up, you are better able to notice opportunities as they appear.

Not only can we keep our eyes open, we can keep our minds open. Have you ever noticed a thought passing through your head, perhaps the thought of an old friend whom you haven't spoken to in years? You have the choice of ignoring that thought or acting on it. Why not contact that person and let her know that you were thinking of her? Maybe she is experiencing a challenge in her life and could use some support. Or maybe she has had some good fortune and you could share in her joy! It's your choice, call her or ignore the thought of her.

Take note tomorrow when you wake up. Do you slump over and say, "Good God—morning..." or do you straighten up, raise your arms and exclaim "Good morning, God!"?

Your attitude determines your altitude. How much joy and happiness do you want to let into your life? You are the one who makes that determination! Try taking off your blinders and put up your antennas. You are sure to discover a tremendous bounty of goodness that life has to offer!

21

Who's Responsible?

Accountability is one characteristic of happy people that I discuss in my program, *Simple Happiness*. If you are to be a truly happy person, you must come to the realization that the person you are today is the result of all the choices you've ever made in your life. No excuses, no blame, it's all your own doing. At first, this might seem terrifying. On the other hand, it can be quite an empowering concept: "my life is in my own hands." The choices you make, minute to minute, determine how your life is going to work out.

Do you get up when the alarm clock goes off and take a brisk walk before work, or do you hit the snooze button and go back to sleep? Do you stop to get a donut for breakfast or do you eat a banana instead? Do you give your spouse a hug or do you ignore her? Do you monitor your kids' schoolwork or do you just fly off the handle in anger, surprised when they bring home poor grades? Each and every choice you make carries consequences.

As you go through your day, it can be very productive to observe the choices you are making. Just observe, don't chastise or criticize. Perhaps you will start to realize that you shape your life through what seems to be unimportant events of everyday life.

Jim Rohn, a businessman and motivational speaker once said, "Everything matters." What an awesome and frightening statement. Don't get me wrong. I'm not saying that everyone should have the discipline to run a marathon, or become a concert pianist. But if you look closely, people get where they are because of the choices they make.

As a child, you had to do as you were told. Now as an adult, you're calling the shots. Take notice of your thoughts when things aren't quite working out the way you would like them to. We often opt to lay blame on someone or something else. Notice how easy it is to notice when others make excuses for the way things are. It takes a big person to assume responsibility for the way his life is turning out.

Helen Keller once said, "Self pity is our worst enemy and if we yield to it, we can never do anything wise in this world." We might say to ourselves, "What do you expect? My parents got divorced when I was young" or "My father was an alcoholic." Those statements may be true, but if you intend to make a better life for yourself, you must realize that even though life's circumstances may have affected you, what you do from that point on is up to you! You have the choice to complain about why your life is just average, or you can move forward and start making choices that bring you closer to the life you want to live.

When you can take responsibility for defeats as well as victories, your life will take a major turn for the better.

22

Do You Make the Time?

"I don't have the time." How often in response to a thought of pursuing something we might consider worthwhile or just a lot of fun, have we used these words as an excuse for not getting involved? But really, all we do have is time. We, like everyone else on the planet, have 24 hours every day.

Many of us are always in a rush. In today's world, both parents are busy working, getting the kids off to school, to soccer practice, to dancing lessons and tutoring for the fourth grade achievement tests. We find ourselves spending our time arranging play dates, supervising homework, juggling work and home, and all the other life activities. It is no surprise that we don't find time to do what's really important to us.

Some of us are good at time management. Some are not. Some of us are very organized. Some of us are not. The main question here is: how do you feel about the way things are? You might love the excitement of being always on the move. That's great! But, on the other hand, if you feel pressured by all your daily chores, maybe it is time to step back and consider things.

What do you really miss doing? Relaxing with a good book? Taking a daily walk? Meditating? Spending a little quality time with your spouse? Pursuing your hobby? Joining a club?

There is a risk you run by not making time to do things that are important to you. You might begin to resent some of the things you have to do during the day. There are plenty of books written on time management, if you are inclined to read them. I, like many people, have a lot of responsibilities and a lot of interests. What I've decided to do

> *Let your feelings be your guide.*

is compartmentalize my day. I happen to be a "morning person." I like to take advantage of the quiet time early in the morning before things start to happen. This is my time for exercise, reading and meditating. Then I focus on my work during the day. In the evening, I allocate time for family dinner and other pursuits.

When I divide up my day in this manner, I can see blocks of time to get involved with activities that are important to me. Things don't always unfold as planned, but on most days, I manage to find some time to pursue things that are important to me. Even if things don't work out today, I know that tomorrow I'll be able to have some time for me. If you notice that you rarely have time for yourself, you may consider delegating some tasks and responsibilities to others in the family.

Let your feelings be your guide. If you are happy with your schedule and you look forward to each day with enthusiasm, then why change anything? It's when you begin to feel that you don't have time for yourself that you should step back and consider your alternatives. "I want to bring joy and high spirits to my daily activities, not resentment and the feeling that I'd rather be doing something else." The last thing anyone wants to say in old age, as he or she looks back on life, is, "I didn't have the time to pursue my dreams." Make the time, now!

Are You Painting the Past Blue?

"Bring up the past just to paint it blue," is a noteworthy line from one of James Taylor's songs. How many times has a thought come into your mind about an incident from the past that caused you to feel a little bit sad or upset? I'm sure it happens, at least once in a while.

The next time it happens to you, take notice. Observe what is going on in your head and your heart at that moment. Take a step backward and realize what is happening. You may be experiencing the same emotion that you encountered years ago when the distressing incident took place. It is not taking place now, so why would you want to feel bad all over again?

You may have never even realized that you have the ability to simply recognize the thought and let it go—no emotions attached. You don't have to "bring up the past just to paint it blue." You can heal yourself from past pains by deliberately choosing a better feeling thought about that unpleasant incident, and then move on from it.

To demonstrate this, I sometimes use the analogy of getting a small cut on your arm. It's not life-threatening, just a minor wound. How would you deal with it? You would probably clean it, apply some disinfectant, and put a bandage on it. And then finally, you'd leave it alone and it would heal. A miracle, right?

However, what might happen if you continually removed the bandage to show the cut to everyone you meet? What if you even demonstrated how deep the cut is? You would most likely risk infection and possible further complications—in other words, more pain from the same wound. That is exactly what you are doing to yourself when you dwell on a thought about a hurtful event from your past.

Use this comparison the next time you notice yourself hanging onto an old negative thought. Understand that you have the choice to dwell on the hurts of the past or to recognize the hurtful thought for what it is—just a thought. And then quickly move on to a more empowering, uplifting thought.

When you realize that you have control over your thoughts and their correlating emotions, you just might find yourself happily bringing up your past. Just remember to paint it rosy!

24

Don't Make Assumptions

In the book, The Four Agreements by Don Miguel Ruiz, one of the four agreements is "Don't Make Assumptions." It is a temptation that is very difficult to resist. When faced with disappointment, we tend to try to figure things out. If another person or persons are involved, we feel the need to know what motivated them to act the way they did. We immediately want to jump to conclusions based on what seems evident to us at the time.

Making assumptions is a perfect example of how we let our thoughts get the best of us. When you assume, you take the situation for granted. Your reaction may be unwarranted. That is why it is so important to stop and consider the circumstances before making a judgment call. If you are feeling offended or disappointed, you need to determine if your emotional response is valid or merely a quick reflex. Someone once said, "When you assume, you make an 'ass' out of 'u' and 'me'". This means that assumptions lack the proof or support of the response.

Don't forget, it's not what happens to us that makes the difference; it is how we deal with what happens to us.

When you make an assumption about someone or something, it usually means you are feeling the need to take it upon yourself to take action or make a decision as only you see fit. Your perspective is usually clouded, but your emotional attachment to the situation keeps the snow ball effect going. One assumption leads to another. The reality of the situation or the truth about someone becomes lost in your view of things. If an assumption has caused you negative feelings, this kind of false thinking can put you into a downward spiral! You waste vital energy focusing on your assumption, holding yourself in a negative state. You might spend an entire day planning what you will say to the person who disappointed you or how you will make right your perceived wrong-doing. These negative thoughts compel us to try to find a way to immediately rectify the situation to our advantage, which may not be the correct thing to do.

In a circumstance where we are upset but don't have all the facts, we have the option of waiting until we've cooled down a bit. It's really amazing how a little time and distance from a situation can help put things into perspective. Somehow, on the next day, we don't feel quite as affected as we did the day before. Also, when we are in a better mood, if the event is still an issue, we have a much better chance of finding the right words to get our point across. Usually the emotion of the moment lessens our ability to communicate in our normally reasonable and productive fashion. Plus, new information is more likely to be revealed at a later point, which could bring a new light to the situation.

Once again, the trick is to notice things as they are happening. Making assumptions, in this case, negative assumptions, is a sure way to keep you from your happiness. We never really know what is going on inside someone else. When you find yourself disheartened about someone, it is usually your own confusion that triggers you to make an assumption about them, which in most cases is not true. Your assumption may be concluded because of something negative that was factual in the past, and those former disappointments activate a thought of "here we go again." But just because we may have been right in the past, does not mean that we are right in the present. Sometimes feelings of dismay are the result of an honest misunderstanding. Other times, our distress might stem from being too sensitive. In any event, it is always wise to take a step back to see the bigger picture in any situation. There is always more than meets the eye, which when seen clearly, can spare unnecessary hurt.

Take notice when you are in the act of making an assumption. You'll be surprised how often you do. Notice the empowerment you feel as you make the choice to give others the benefit of the doubt.

Things to Do

25

Appreciate, Appreciate, Appreciate

One of the fundamental concepts in living a happy life is that our lives are really a series of choices. We are constantly making choices. Most of the time, the choices we make today are pretty much the same as the ones we made yesterday. If we want to have a happier, more fulfilling life, it makes sense that we must make some changes in our choices.

A very simple choice that can make a huge difference is choosing to appreciate. That's right, appreciating is a choice. What is the opposite of appreciation? I know what you are thinking—"depreciation." You're right, but for our purposes, the choice is either to appreciate or take for granted. We all take things for granted! If you want to make a change, the first step is to notice your thoughts. What is your first thought as you slide your legs over the side of your bed as you get up? Probably the same thing you thought yesterday, whatever that was. How about an act of appreciation: "Thank God I can get out of the bed by myself"? One day, you might not be able to accomplish this simple act. Appreciate your good health now!

What do you think as you slowly make your way into the bathroom? You have the choice to say to yourself, "Thank God I have indoor plumbing." How many people in the world do not have indoor plumbing? This simple thought of appreciation can point you in a positive direction for the day. Once, when I was making this point at one of my talks, a woman called out, "Thank God my plumbing works!" Do you take for granted the wonders of the inner workings of your body? You probably do. Most of us only think about the miracle of our bodies when something goes wrong. Like this woman, we have a choice to appreciate the basics of life.

All through the day there are opportunities to appreciate. It is a conscious choice. As you practice appreciating the moments of your day, you will notice yourself enjoying yourself a bit more. Just like hanging on to a negative thought can put us on a downward spiral of feeling bad, hanging on to a thought of appreciation can lead to another thought of appreciation, and another, and so on. We can put ourselves in an upward spiral.

We hear a lot about the benefits of living in the present moment. I really believe that the choice to appreciate versus taking things for granted does just that. The act of appreciation brings us into awareness of the present moment where we can feel joy in what we are doing now.

It's up to you! You have the power to turn your life in the direction of sadness or in the direction of happiness. Appreciate, appreciate, appreciate... and your life will be happier!

26

Follow Your Bliss

I was watching an interview on PBS some time ago. Bill Moyers was interviewing Joseph Campbell, a world-renowned expert in Religion and Mythology. At one point in the interview, Joseph Campbell said, "If you follow your bliss, doors will open that you didn't even know existed." I quickly sat up in my chair and took notice. What a mind-boggling concept! To follow your bliss! What is your bliss? It is that which makes you feel most alive. It is, perhaps, an activity where time passes without your noticing it. Your bliss is when you feel no stress—just fulfillment.

"Doors will open that you didn't even know existed." That statement captures the realization that there are things that you don't even know that you don't know! As you follow your bliss, new opportunities are waiting to reveal themselves to you. There are ideas that as of yet, you haven't even thought about. As you follow your bliss, your consciousness will be expanded. Your talents will become developed and you will naturally share in your gifts. As you follow your bliss, your life becomes more meaningful and fulfilled.

Most of us live our lives safely inside our comfort zone, venturing just so far, but not too far away from safety. Why won't we venture outside of our comfort zone? When I ask this question at my talks, most answers contain the words "fear" or "afraid." Sometimes it's too much responsibility, lack of time or just plain laziness. Whatever our reasons, most of us find an excuse for not following our bliss.

Often we are discouraged from following our bliss by those closest to us, our friends or our family. They like us the way we are or perhaps fear that

When you follow your bliss, great opportunities come your way.

they will be left behind if we begin to make more of ourselves. Our family may be motivated to protect us from making a big mistake or from failing, but if we have the intention to follow our bliss, we must, as Wayne Dyer says, "Have a healthy disregard for the good opinion of others."

If we can wade through the negativity of others and give up our own excuses, then stepping out of our comfort zone can be an exhilarating experience, not a terrifying one. As we overcome the fear of being vulnerable, risking failure and ridicule, or the "I told you so's," and move into the direction of our bliss, doors do start to open that we didn't know existed. It is only then that we begin to understand that this is how our life was supposed to be lived.

When you follow your bliss, great opportunities come your way. Situations or challenges begin to work in your favor. People show up to encourage you and reveal new ideas. Certain books or tapes find you that explain things in a new light. You start to experience an inner courage that you didn't know you had. You begin to feel more alive. Your purpose on earth becomes clearer. You start living your life on a new, exciting level.

Take the chance, follow your bliss... It's worth it!

27

Pay It Forward

Sometimes a small turn in consciousness can make a big difference. Often when we think about making changes so we can live a fuller, happier, more meaningful life, we shy away because we think it's going to be difficult and frustrating. We figure we'll end up back where we started anyway. But sometimes we can start with just a small idea. Sometimes a small change can have a big effect!

What do you want to do when someone does a favor for you? You are probably grateful for the kind deed and then look for an opportunity to repay the favor to even the score.

An example of a small turn in consciousness that can make a big difference was played out in the movie after which this chapter is entitled. It was presented as an idea that can change the world. When someone does a favor for you, instead of paying him back, your job is to do something nice for three other people. In the movie, it is explained as three big things, but for us it could be three small things.

Consider the concept of "paying it forward" in your life. The initial favor could be as simple as someone telling you that you left your lights on as you get out of your car in the parking lot. That kind deed sets your mind to be ready to do something nice for three other people as soon as the opportunity presents itself. Paying it forward could be as effortless as allowing someone ahead of you in the checkout line who has a small child or a few items in their wagon. It could be a friendly wave allowing a car into traffic or offering to help an older neighbor shovel snow.

This gentle turn in consciousness encourages us to live more in the present moment—noticing the favor, being grateful and then consciously looking for opportunities to pass the kindness along to others. The simple act of noticing thoughtful acts, followed by a deliberate decision to be good to others can have a huge impact in how we live our lives. Developing a conscious habit of seeking out opportunities to be kind could be the first step on your path toward living a fuller, happier, more meaningful life.

This book is my kind deed to you. Now it's your turn to pay it forward!

28

Enjoy Creation

We live in a very high tech, sophisticated world. Sometimes we think we have it all figured out. We have come so far, learned so much. We identify ourselves by how much we earn, where we live, what colleges our children attend, and so on. We also live in a society of fear, fighting disease, terrorism and loss of our lives or possessions. By leaning too much on our material success and dwelling on living in fear, we run the risk of losing our balance.

Balance can be achieved by enjoying creation. Look at the world as though you are looking through the eyes of a child. Be in awe of nature. Certainly there must be a higher power behind it all! We can choose to take creation for granted or we can derive a deep sense of joy from being a small part of this amazing universe.

Fill yourself with the wonders of creation. Experience the power of a thunderstorm, the brilliant colors of a sunset, and the extraordinary order of day following night or spring following winter. What about the leaves falling off the trees in the autumn? How do all the rivers keep flowing? That's a lot of water! Look at where the sun rises in the summer and compare that to where it rises in the winter. Smell a rose, honeysuckle or a lily. Why does the moon look so huge sometimes as it rises in the east? Why do cows eat grass and tigers eat meat? How can a tree grow out of a rock? How far away are the stars? How do fish breathe? How do robins know where the worms are? How do squirrels remember where they buried their acorns? Why are there waves in the ocean? What's the story with the tides? These are just a few questions that cross my mind from time to time. The point is that we have the ability to enjoy all that exists in the universe.

There are many miracles of nature just waiting to bring harmony into our fast-paced, problem-filled lives. The practice of noticing these wonders of creation will bring the balance you seek and offer a new perspective to cope in whatever world you choose to see yourself in.

29

Feed Your Mind

W e all know that nourishment is essential to life. Everyday we must eat and drink. Sure, we can go without food and water for a time, but without nourishment our bodies will shut down.

In order to avoid starvation, our bodies are equipped with sensors that tell us we need to drink, (we feel thirsty), and we need to eat, (we feel hungry). How we satisfy that hunger and thirst will have a lasting effect on our health and our quality of life. Eating the right foods can help produce a healthy, vigorous body, which can serve us for many years to come. Eating the wrong foods can lead us to a body more prone to various medical problems. In general, most of us know that in order to be healthy we must feed our bodies well.

It is a very different story when it comes to the mind. Daily attention to feeding the mind is not essential to living. It is possible to live without ever venturing out of your little world, where you think the same thoughts day after day.

Is that really living? On a certain level, it is. However, we, as humans, are called to a higher life. We are called, but sometimes we don't pay any attention to the call.

We need to experience some kind of spark to ignite our desire to grow, learn and develop the potential we have inside us. Just like a campfire, if we want to keep it burning, we must continually add wood. So too, our inner fire must continually be fed as well.

Reading is an excellent source of food for the mind. You can get a book on almost any subject, which can inspire and excite you. The ideas they bring can show you new ways of looking at many things. Reading can open doors that you didn't even know existed. It's the expansion of ideas that is so important. What you do with those ideas is up to you.

There is a smorgasbord of mind food available to us. It might be a biography, a non-fiction book, a novel with characters that inspire you or perhaps a self-help book. It can even be a magazine or a short newspaper article on a topic that interests you. In today's mind kitchen, there is a wide selection of other media dishes to chow down on: audios, videos, movies, and the Internet. Of course, there are workshops, lectures, or even continuing education classes that serve up a hearty meal for the mind.

Remember, like choosing healthy foods for the body, it is important to nourish the mind with information that will benefit your thinking for the long haul.

As the saying goes, "A mind is a terrible thing to waste!"
What's on your plate?

30

Volunteer

One of the necessary keys for a life of joy and fulfillment is giving of yourself in some way so that someone else's life might be better. Often, we think of giving only as a monetary contribution to a charity. Monetary gifts are certainly an extremely important aspect of giving, however, being charitable through your time and talents offers a more profound personal experience for both the giver and the receiver.

It is written in the ancient sacred scriptures of the Talmud that the reward of charity depends entirely upon the extent of the kindness in it. That means that the greatest gift is the one that we give out of the pure hope that someone's life may be better. We do not look for a pat on the back or any other reward.

In some churches, they refer to this concept as stewardship- giving of time and talent. That is the beauty of the universe. There are so many people with different talents. We often use these talents in the workplace through our careers. Some of us have talents that aren't really maximized in our jobs. What better place to use these talents than in helping others?

We get so caught up in our own little worlds that we lose sight of what's going on around us. Though many of us are blessed in so many ways, others are not doing so well. There are those who experience personal sadness, loneliness, disappointment and frustration. They feel that there is no way out, that life is leaving them behind.

Coming from either end of the scale, volunteering can be such an uplifting and healing experience. For those who are blessed, volunteering can give them a chance to experience life's higher purpose. For those who are feeling down, volunteering is a chance to gain perspective. It can lift them out of a depressed state by realizing that others have it worse than themselves.

That's what giving of your time and talent does. We start to experience the joy of selfless giving. Further, we begin to realize that there are many others who are doing the same thing; giving selflessly to others. We begin to see that the world is made of many fine people who are doing their best to make this a better place: it's not necessarily the negative world that the TV news portrays.

Many of us think that we don't have the time to volunteer. It's true that our lives are busy. However, you will find that when you step outside your little world to give to others, you will come back to your world better equipped to love, lead and inspire those around you.

Start as Soon as You Wake Up

Whether you're a morning person or a night person, your day starts as soon as you wake up! That's the perfect time to reach for the best feeling thought you can find!

Most of us live in a daily routine, pretty much doing the same things every day. Why not add something to your schedule that will get you off to a great start each day? Get in the habit of giving thanks for the gift of life as soon as you wake up!

I heard a story once that made me feel sad, happy, and somewhat upset all at the same time. A young woman experiencing headaches was told after seeing several doctors that she had brain cancer and only had two weeks to live. Imagine the horror of being told such a thing! How sad to have your life cut down, just like that. She was, of course, devastated. But then, after further testing, it was revealed that it was not brain cancer at all. It turns out it was only an infection that had gone to her brain as a "freaky" result of recent

dental work. Her newly diagnosed condition was cured by a simple regime of antibiotics. Can you imagine the relief she must have felt? The young woman had been granted a new lease on life.

From then on, the woman began to look at her life in a whole new way. She now greets each day as if it were a miraculous gift to her. She makes an effort to live everyday to its fullest—feeling happy to be alive and well!

The truly upsetting part of this story was my realization that so many people need a near-death experience to really be thankful for their lives. It takes a major crisis, like a brick over the head, for them to begin welcoming each day as the precious gift it is. It's sad to think there are people who never feel the pure exhilaration of being alive like that woman now feels. I wonder how many people are just "existing" and not really valuing the miracle of life. The truth is that far too many are. But it could be different. It's simply a matter of bringing the miracle of life to mind the moment we rise to meet each day.

Tomorrow, as you awaken, take a nice deep breath and be thankful for the miraculous gift just given to you. Forget your troubles. Shake off any stress. Tell yourself, "I can face anything! I've done it before and I can do it again." My guess is that if you welcome each day with a renewed sense of excitement and appreciation, your worries will soon melt away and miracles will begin to take their place. Thankfulness—start as soon as you wake up!

32

Lighten Up

Many of us want to live a life of peace, joy and happiness. We look high and low for answers without satisfaction. Some of us spend a great deal of energy on the need to be right. In response to another's statement, we say things like, "That's ridiculous," "Where did you hear that," or "How could that be?" We shoot their opinions or thoughts down when they don't agree with ours. What's the big deal in allowing someone else to be right once in awhile? Ask yourself this question: "Is it more important for me to be right or to be kind?" If your gut response is that you want to be right, than perhaps it's time you lightened up! You don't always have to take yourself so seriously!

When you are at a party or a gathering of some kind, do you really listen to what others are saying or are you just looking for a place to jump in and tell your story? Try to let someone else have the floor. Let someone else be the center of attention.

Maybe you're someone who is always looking to be

offended! Your conversations center on what others did that rubbed you the wrong way. You can't wait to get to the office to tell everyone how the counterperson messed up your bagel order. You may even boast about how you berated the person in front of the other customers. We all have our moments when we feel the need to show our superiority. It could be the need to criticize or belittle others when they are not present. If you tend to walk around with the proverbial "chip" on your shoulder, you are stuck in your ego!

> *...begin by adding the ingredient of compassion into your daily living.*

There is another way that will lead to a life filled with more peace and joy. But first, you must be aware of how often you feel offended, uptight or righteous. The realization that you have a choice in how you deal with everyday irksome situations can be enlightening. People who are easily offended choose to be. It is not because others are looking to upset them. In every circumstance, irritating or not, you have a choice whether to be bothered or not. How you respond to any situation determines how you will feel afterwards. When confronted with something which might normally anger you, say to yourself, "Next year, will I look back at this situation and think it was important?" The answer is probably not. It is at that moment that you can lighten up by choosing to be kind instead of being right.

If you truly want to be happy, begin by adding the ingredient of compassion into your daily living. Start by catching someone doing something right instead of catching someone doing something wrong. Pay attention to your attitude. Take notice when your ego rears its ugly head. Whenever you start to feel defensive and argumentative, check yourself and choose a lighter response. You'll feel good when your compassionate side wins out over your ego as you notice yourself being less defensive.

As you lighten up, you'll see how you not only bring out the best in yourself, but you also bring out the best in those around you. In my experience, if you want to be happy, first you have to lighten up. And then the Golden Rule is easier to apply!

33

Don't Be Discouraged

How often does this happen: you start on a new regime, whether it's to lose weight, get in shape, read more, quit smoking, be more organized, or whatever, and before you know it, you've fallen back into your old ways? It's not easy to make changes in your life. It can be frustrating not to get to where you want to be.

Don't be discouraged! Everyday is another chance to start again. Yesterday's failure could be today's breakthrough! Success for many of us is like opening a combination lock. Let's say you need to hit four numbers so the lock will open. If you have two numbers, it won't open. If you have three numbers, it still won't open. All you need to do is find that fourth number. And then— hooray! The lock opens! In our efforts to change or try new things, most people manage to get to numbers two or three. Then, before going for the fourth, they give up. When you feel like you want to give up, that's when you shouldn't get discouraged. The fourth number is just waiting for you to keep trying!

Here are a couple of images to bring to mind when you're considering throwing in the towel. The first is, "How long do we give a baby to learn how to walk?" Imagine if a mother and father would say to each other, "Okay, we've already been teaching the baby to walk for three weeks now and he's already sixteen months old. Forget it, he'll never walk!" What's the possibility of parents saying that? None; they will keep working with the baby for as long as it takes until he can walk.

The second image is the "ant theory." We've all seen an ant walking along the ground with a little white speck in his mouth. What will the ant do if you place a stick in his way? That's right; he'll walk over or around it. What will he do if you place two sticks in his way? Right again! He still goes over or around them. What's the only way to stop an ant from getting where he wants to go? By stepping on him! In other words, it means he can be stopped only through an extreme external force. So why is it that people, the highest form of life on the planet, give up so easily?

Life certainly has many challenges, but it also rewards us as we move through them. You are here to live as happy as you see fit for you, no matter what outside influences or obstacles come your way. So don't be discouraged. The next number just may be your fourth! And then— hooray! You unlock your potential!

34

Visualize

In another chapter we talked about the concept that our lives become what we think about all day long. I can't emphasize enough the importance of noticing what is going on in your head. As you become more aware of your thoughts, you can begin to steer them in the direction of what you want your life to be by envisioning the outcome.

Visualization is a deliberate focus on whatever image you want to hold in your mind. As you choose to hang on to empowering thoughts, you begin to manifest life in a way that matches your thoughts. William James, the Father of American psychology, who lived from 1842-1910, put it this way, "There is a law in psychology that if you form a picture in your mind of what you would like to be, and you keep and hold that picture there long enough, you will soon become exactly as you have been thinking." What a powerful concept, indeed!

I read the book many years ago called "Psycho-Cybernetics" by plastic surgeon, Dr. Maxwell Maltz.

In those days, the focus of plastic surgery was to repair deformities and not for cosmetic purposes. However, Dr. Maltz began to notice remarkable changes in the personalities of the patients who had undergone corrective surgeries. These positive changes could be traced to how the patients felt about their improved looks. Dr. Maltz further considered that it would be wonderful if positive changes could be made without surgery, just by visualization. He conducted a simple experiment by going to a local college and gathering thirty volunteers from a men's physical education class. He had them each shoot twenty-five foul shots. Now some of the young men were skilled basketball players and some were not. They tallied up the scores and the average for the group was eight out of twenty-five.

The men were then divided randomly into three groups of ten. The assignment for the first group was to come to the gym everyday for a month and shoot 50 foul shots. The second group was instructed to do nothing that was different from their normal routine. If they played basketball, they should keep doing it. If they never touched a ball, they should just continue to do the same. The third group was instructed to spend ten minutes each day for the same thirty days, visualizing themselves at the gym, standing at the foul line and making shot after shot. They were to visualize a perfect shot each time, touching only the net. They were instructed to never actually touch a ball, just picture the perfect result.

After thirty days, they all came back to the gym and each shot twenty-five foul shots. The results were amazing! The first group who practiced everyday saw their average go up from eight shots to twelve shots. The second group remained the same. But the third group that only practiced visualization also improved their average to twelve shots made. They did just as well as those who had actually practiced. Final analysis: less physical work, same results.

The bottom-line is that our thoughts do create our reality. That is why it is so important to be aware of thoughts that we do not want or that make us feel bad. The ego-mind likes to wander away from your best intention. It takes practice to manage your thoughts to keep them focused on your desired goal. Using visualization exercises will help tame your thoughts and keep them on track. It is a perfect tool to use to take control of your life. Decide what you want and start spending time each day picturing the desired result in your mind. Make a point of bringing it to mind often throughout the day. It sometimes helps to cut out pictures and post them around your home or workspace as a reminder. Simply envision your success. Notice how good it feels to achieve what you want. Then just relax and allow it to happen. What you see will eventually be what you get!

As with the experiment above, it's important to

first know what you want to accomplish. Next, spend time visualizing the end result. Then just relax and wait until the moment is right to take appropriate action.

Isn't it time you visualized your dreams into reality?

35

You Can Meditate

The French philosopher Blaise Pascal said, "All man's miseries derive from not being able to sit quietly in a room alone." Many of us spend most of our waking moments occupied with all kinds of concerns, problems and stresses. We are constantly filling our lives with distractions—radio, TV, computer, you name it! People today are always on the go and hardly spend any tranquil time by themselves.

If you want to effect change in your life you must change something. I have been talking about the many ways in which you can adjust your thinking by make small turns in consciousness. Here, I suggest that you introduce a non-activity into your daily routine called meditation. And it's guaranteed to pay high dividends!

"Me? Mediate?" you say! Yes, everyone can learn to meditate. And you don't need a lot of time either—only five or ten minutes.

Find a moment during the day when you can sit in a quiet place by yourself without interruptions. No radio, no TV, no cell phone, no kids—just you. I understand that this in itself may be a challenge for you. You will soon see that it is worth it!

As you sit silently with your eyes closed, simply breathe. Notice your chest expanding and the way your diaphragm helps to increase your breathing capacity. Feel the air filling your lungs. Then let the air out. Maybe you'll breathe a bit deeper than usual. That's fine. As you continue to breathe, you will notice thoughts entering your consciousness. Merely identify them as thoughts and let them go. Get back to your breathing. More thoughts will come. Each time release them and keep coming back to your breathing. Some people like to have a mantra—some sound or word that they say to themselves to help bring them back to their quiet state.

If you want to effect change in your life, you must change something.

This stillness brought about by meditation is your natural state of being. Like Deepak Chopra suggests, we are, after all, "human beings, not human doings." Meditation allows you to be a human just being. Doing nothing! From a place of inner calmness, you will realize and experience your genius self. Infinite ideas, creativity, solutions and empowering wisdom are just beneath what you have been covering up with outside noise.

One day while meditating, the solution to a problem that has been bothering you, may suddenly appear to you. A great idea about how you can express your love to your spouse or children may show up. You may discover a hidden talent or release an ongoing creative block.

It's amazing what will happen if you stick to a meditation practice. Many surprising things will make themselves known to you. Start small, a minute or two. If you wake-up a few minutes earlier than usual, sit and breathe before starting your day. Perhaps at lunch you can go sit in your car for a few minutes, or before you drive home from work. Just find a time and a place where there is little external distraction.

Everything you need for a happy, wonderful life is already inside you. So take time daily to quiet down a bit and allow the hidden inspirations within you to flow. You will reap the fruits of your non-labor tenfold!

36

The Golden Rule

Do you know what the Golden Rule is? It is a fundamental moral principle found in virtually all major religions. It quite simply means, "Treat others the way you want them to treat you." The Golden Rule is the basic directive of how to live your life. "Love thy neighbor as yourself," as written in the Laws of Moses. In Christianity, of which I am most familiar, Jesus says in the Gospels, "Do unto others as you would have them do unto you." As offered by Confucius, "What you do not want others to do to you, do not do to others." Whatever the culture, the words might be different, but the message is the same.

I challenge you to live the Golden Rule. Don't start with your whole life, not even your whole day. It will mean you will have to set aside your ego, which may not be easy for a whole day. So start with little slices of your day. Maybe you could try the first hour at work. You can begin by being conscious of how you treat others. Go quietly about your business as usual, but take interest in all of your personal interactions.

Don't tell anyone what you're up to or expect anything in return. Observe how you feel as you consciously treat others the way you would like them to treat you. And don't expect to be canonized a saint during your first hour—just enjoy the experience!

Little by little, expand your Golden Rule throughout the day. Maybe you could try it on your commute home. Don't make any major changes; simply be yourself with a little expansion in your consciousness. Why not offer a fellow commuter your seat or smile kindly to a homeless person huddled in the corner of the subway. Perhaps you could let a car ahead of you as you are driving in bumper to bumper traffic. The idea is to recognize how you are feeling as you behave thoughtfully to others and to see how they are responding.

Later when you are alone, ask yourself how you like to be treated. Do you like it when people respect you, even your superiors? Do you like it when you are shown patience as you struggle through a task? Do you like it when people are interested in what you have to say? Do you like it when people take an interest in your family? Do you like it when people compliment you? The answers to these questions will guide you as to how to treat others.

Living the Golden Rule is a very simple concept with a very powerful result. However, it is not always easy to put into practice. We often walk around in our egos, which are filled with self-importance. We think we are superior over others or feel the need to be right. We convince ourselves that we have an image to uphold. The ego likes to take charge of our attitude and dictate our every action. It distracts us from the truth about who we are and what we truly want. The basis of the Golden Rule represents the complete opposite.

Make a point to follow the Golden Rule everyday. Let the ego go once in a while. Don't take yourself so seriously or look to be offended by the actions of others. Instead, seek out ways to love, respect and show consideration to those who come your way. You will soon see that living by the Golden Rule has one distinct end result—inner peace. And that is as *golden* as it gets!

Strategies

37

Is Someone Living in Your Head Rent Free?

D o you ever get a thought in your head about something somebody did or said to you years ago that hurt your feelings? Maybe you didn't get invited to a party or maybe your kids didn't get invited. Do you usually hang on to a thought like that and start to feel bad? Do you relive the hurt all over again? Does it start you on a downward spiral of negative emotions? If you do, it's your own fault! Do you think the person who caused the hurt has given it another thought? Probably not! Here you are, feeling hurt all over again. Why?

Wayne Dyer says that the past is like the wake of a boat—the trail the boat leaves as it travels through the water. It shows where the boat has been. Does the wake of the boat have any control over the captain who is navigating the boat? No, of course not!

If you can notice yourself hanging onto that negative thought before it takes a downward spiral, you could avoid unnecessarily feeling bad. It is your choice. Just as the wake of the boat has no real control over the present direction of the boat, your past has no real control over what you are doing at the present time. Unless you let the past have control.

I find that mental images sometimes help us in our efforts to live a happier life. One night at one of my talks, when I was discussing negative feelings that recur and make us feel bad, a woman in the audience raised her hand and said, "Do you know what it's like when you let something that somebody did years ago continue to bother you? It's like letting her live in your head rent-free." Wow, that's a powerful picture!

The first step is to be aware of your thoughts and the accompanying negative feelings. As you do, you can choose to let that thought go as you recall the idea of the wake of the boat and the rent-free tenant. You can take control and not let that disempowering thought take over. You'll be able to acknowledge your thought and identify it as just a thought; not as something that is happening in your life right now. You will be able to replace that thought with an empowering thought and triumphantly move on. This whole process may take place in a split second and may not seem to be that big a deal, but these small private victories can help reshape our lives.

When you find yourself thinking uncomfortable thoughts, evict them by replacing them with the next best feeling thought. After all, you are the landlord of your thoughts!

Have a Healthy Disregard for the Good Opinion of Others

Why do we stay in our comfort zone? What keeps us from following our bliss? What prevents us from breaking out and achieving our full potential? Though there are many valid answers to these questions, there is one worth addressing here: the influence of others. Often, it is the people around us who discourage us from making changes in our lives, even those that benefit us.

People might say things like, "Are you sure you want to take a chance?" or "What will people say if it doesn't work out?" or "Who do you think you are to try that?" Sometimes the discouraging words come from people closest to us, our friends and even our family. These discouraging words can really take the wind out of our sails.

Notice the title of this chapter says to have a healthy disregard for the "good" opinion of others. Often the words of discouragement are not meant in a mean way.

Our discouragers may really not want us to get hurt or make a real mistake. However, sometimes without even realizing it, their words of gloom come from the fear that if you go ahead and do what you intend to do, it might have an affect on them. Perhaps they feel you may leave them behind or that they may lose you as a friend. It could also be that they simply like you the way you are, even if it is not who you want to be. For some, your progress highlights their weaknesses, which may leave them feeling that you believe that you are better than they are!

Stepping out of your comfort zone is difficult enough without the significant pressure that often comes from those around you. None of us likes to hear, "I told you so!" The reality is that when you take chances and pursue the life of your dreams, you are really encouraging those around you to do the same. It is said that when we look back over our lives, we don't regret the things we did, but we regret the things we didn't do!

A true friend is one who wants you to be all that you can be. A true friend is one who challenges you, pushes you and encourages you to do and be more. A true friend also allows you to find your own way, even if it means making a mistake. It is the fortunate person who has that kind of friend and can be one as well.

The road to overcoming insecurities or lack of self-confidence is tough enough. When you find that you are ready to take that extra step out of the box, be prepared for the inevitable naysayers ready to dissuade you. You might politely listen to their points of view. Perhaps even consider their advice. But in the end, a healthy disregard for the good opinion of others often leads to success!

Relax—You May Only Have a Few Minutes Left

This line is the title of a wonderful book by Loretta Laroche. Her angle is using humor to reduce the negative effects of stress—death being one of them. Some people think that focusing on death is morbid, unproductive and just plain scary. Loretta Laroche and I take the opposite view. In another chapter I wrote about the many benefits that can be had by realizing that we will probably live a long life. There is one undisputable fact, however. We are all going to die someday—no doubt, no possible arguments.

This realization that death is certain can be a doubled-edged sword. You could look at it with fear and trepidation. Or you could look at death as a motivator. Thinking about my inescapable death makes me think more about what I'm doing with my life today, while I'm still alive. Considering your death can yield some very positive results.

Just think if this were to be your last day on earth.

How would you like to go out? Wouldn't you like to tell your parents how much they have meant to you? Wouldn't you tell your spouse how much you love him or her? How about your kids? Maybe you'd give them a big hug and tell them how proud you are of them. Maybe you'd be a bit more patient and encouraging with them. Would you spend your last day stressed out about a deadline at work or upset about your neighbor's barking dog?

Not that you should throw all your cares to the wind, but considering that this day might be your last day, could lend a little perspective to things. It could help you realize what really matters to you. There are very few people, who, on their deathbeds, sincerely wish that they had spent more time at the office!

The strategy of considering your death to give you new perspective is easier than it sounds. Change is possible. "Relax; you may only have a few minutes left!" So, why not start now! Let joy in. Give the old grim reaper the boot! Carpe Diem—seize the day! This very moment is your chance to express love to those around you, and to reach your fullest potential.

40

God Loves You as Much as He Loves Me

Most of the insights I am sharing with you are borrowed from other people I have come across along my path of personal development and joyful living. In my own quest for simple happiness, I discovered my own little phrase that helps when things get rough or when I am feeling negative emotion towards others. It's a simple thought, "God loves that person as much as He loves me."

Our lives are a series of circumstances that we encounter throughout our day and responses they elicit from us. It is in these responses that we shape our lives. Many of us get into the habit of looking to be offended, whether it's on the highway, in the parking lot at the mall, at the supermarket or even at a soccer game. Take notice the next time you take offense at the actions of another. It is at that moment that you can affirm to yourself, "God loves that person as much as He loves me." You will be pleasantly surprised at how much it defuses your irritation. Once you begin to notice how you are responding to an annoying circumstance, you create a space that allows you to choose how you will react.

In an irksome situation, you can choose to be annoyed and send out anger or you can choose to be compassionate and send love. Being conscious of the present moment, you will be able to catch yourself before reacting negatively. My little phrase, "God loves that person as much as He loves me" is a type of switch that shifts your attention off yourself and onto the other person. You begin to realize that he is a person just like you. You don't know what might be going on in his life that may have caused his negative attitude or behavior. You can choose to give him the benefit of the doubt.

"God loves that person just as much as He loves me," is not reserved for annoying situations. The phrase goes well with everyone who crosses your path. Bringing this phrase to mind often can help to keep us in the present moment, give us perspective and keep us focused on our purpose. Mundane tasks such as going to the bank and the post office or getting gas can take on new meaning.

The next time you interact with someone who's irritating you, take a moment to think, "God loves that person as much as He loves me." You will have chosen peace in the situation and send out love.

41

This is the Day the Lord Has Made

"*This is the day the Lord has made, let us rejoice and be glad in it.*" (Psalm 118:24)

Imagine what a difference your life might be just by saying this simple statement everyday as you awaken. It could set a positive tone for everything that happens throughout your day. This one small turn in consciousness could give you the power to turn an ordinary day into an extraordinary day filled with opportunities for joy. It might help you enjoy that first cup of coffee a little more than usual. You might give your kids a big hug and a kiss and some encouraging words to send them on their way. Perhaps you notice and wave to your neighbor as you pull your car slowly out of the driveway. As you rejoice in your day, you energize yourself and all those with whom you come in contact.

The first part of this phrase, "This is the day the Lord has made," means this is your life now- created just for you. Most of us get caught up in a daily routine; day after day we do some of the same things. We forget each day is a brand new opportunity to make it our own. "Let me just get through it without causing any problems. Let me just get home, have a bite to eat, put on my jammies and get comfortable in front of the TV." Having a routine, in itself, is not a bad thing. But, if your life is dragging and you don't feel as happy as you'd like to be, understand that it is your choice. Often, the only one stopping you from adding joy to your life each day is you!

It's not necessarily what we do during the day that is the most important thing. It's the attitude we bring to those activities that makes the difference. "Let us rejoice and be glad in it." As Mother Theresa of Calcutta said, "We are not all called to do great things, but we are all called to do things with great Love." What a wonderful word "rejoice" is. It means to experience joy again! Experiencing the simple joys of living is so within our reach. We have various frequencies to which we tune our lives. It's just like tuning into a station on the radio. We have the choice of tuning into the news, sports talk, jazz, soft rock, oldies, country—you name it, we can tune into it. It's the same with our lives. We can tune in to negativity, boredom, resentment, looking to be offended, or we can raise our frequency and tune into joy.

It's as easy as setting your daily dial to "This is the day the Lord has made, let us rejoice and be glad in it." You may have to adjust your tuner throughout the day, but you will find that joy is always at the top of your dial.

42

Four Assumptions

While reading Stephen Covey's latest book, *The 8th Habit: From Effectiveness to Greatness*, I discovered four beneficial assumptions that change the way you think about life.

1. **Assume you've had a heart attack; now live accordingly.**

Like those who change the way they perceive life after experiencing a death, we can apply the same principle to the way in which a heart attack might influence you to live a healthier lifestyle. Many of us live as if we were invincible. Certainly, if you were to experience a tightening in your chest and a sharp shooting pain down your arm, all of a sudden things would have to change. You might then decide it is worth the trouble to eat more fruits and vegetables or that it's not so impossible to start an exercise regime. You'd wonder if the stress at work is really worth it. Why not *pretend* that you've already had a heart attack and choose a healthy lifestyle now?

2. Assume the half-life of your profession is two years; now prepare accordingly.

What if you knew that you only had two years to work? Wouldn't that make you more creative and innovative? You might incorporate the 80/20 rule of time management by focusing more on 20 percent of your effort, producing 80 percent of the results. Perhaps you would decide on an entirely different profession, one you always wanted to do. Consider now how you could be more effective at work or what job would really excite you... and do it!

...the only one stopping you from adding joy to your life each day is you!

3. Assume everything you say about another, they can overhear; now speak accordingly.

Speaking negatively about others when they're not around is one of the least worthwhile activities we can engage ourselves in; however, we often do find ourselves speaking ill about others or being subjected to others doing it. The next time it happens, consider the feelings of the absent person or at least walk away when the conservation turns to gossip. There's no need to make an issue of it; simply by choosing not to participate, you make a compassionate statement. Remember the golden rule: Treat others the way you'd like them to treat you, even if they are not around.

4.   Assume you have a one-on-one visit with your Creator every quarter; now live accordingly.

If you actually met with your Creator every quarter, it would undoubtedly be a real consciousness raiser. Most likely, you would avoid the negatives in your life and more clearly understand how to use your gifts and talents for the betterment of yourself and the world. It would be sort of a power-visit whereby you would be reminded of your true value. You would be inspired to live your life always doing your best so that you would have good things to report.

Applying the four assumptions can help keep you focused on the present moment—what is going on right now concerning your body, mind, heart and spirit. And by being in your NOW, you will experience the real meaning of life!

43

Living in the Present Moment

"Living in the present moment" is an expression we have all heard, but what does it really mean? It means noticing where you are right now—being aware of everything that happens, as it is happening. Living in the present moment requires that an inner part of us be able to step back from the external part of our lives to simply observe the experience. When we become the observer, we rise above our physical self to allow a heightened sense of what is taking place. This is not to criticize or chastise ourselves, but to experience being an impartial spectator, simply enjoying life as it is unfolding before us.

It takes the practice of mindfulness to notice what is going on right here and now in our experience. We get so caught up in our thoughts and emotions that they become our lives. Our state of mind—feeling happy or sad, stress or joy—depends upon what thought happens to occupy our mind at the time. Like robots, we automatically become lost in the habitual tendencies that run our lives. Stuck in either dwelling on the past or anxiously anticipating the future, our runaway thoughts keep us from being mindfully aware of what's really going on. To be in the moment, you must separate yourself from incessant thinking about the past or the future. When you are mindful, your natural state of being emerges. Your thoughts begin to unfold in a logical, organic way, moment by moment. When you are in your present moment, you lose any sense of time and space. It is your place of power. All that is real resides there.

The implication here is that living in the present moment is a good thing. And it is. The reality is that it's actually where life is taking place, whether you think so or not. You just might not be recognizing it when you are not in it. Living in the moment simply represents a state of being in authentic awareness.

Let's take a further look at what living in the present moment is not. It's not about the painful experiences of yesterday. It is not old, negative thoughts and it is definitely not fretting about what might have been. You are not in the present moment when you are worrying about a later date, expecting the worst outcome in a situation or feeling concerned about what the future might be. It's important to know that there's nothing wrong with remembering a happy experience from the past or being excited about an upcoming event. These types of thoughts take mindfulness and bring good feelings in the moment. Negative thoughts stem from unconscious thinking, which is why we can't always control them when they surface from time to time. The point is that by choosing to live in the present moment, we become aware of what thoughts occupy our minds in any given point in time. As we knowingly realize we are thinking of the past or future, we instantly bring ourselves back into the present moment. The practice of mindfulness helps us to hang onto the thoughts that are empowering and let go of the thoughts that are disempowering.

Over the years, in my own personal development, I have found great use for memorizing quotes to help keep me on track. I use many of them in my speeches and in this book. To assist you with staying in the present moment, here are a few quotes you might like to commit to memory.

"You cannot change the past, but you can ruin the present by worrying over the future."

—AUTHOR UNKNOWN

"...this moment is the only physical reality you have."

—FROM *REAL MAGIC* BY WAYNE DYER

"Yesterday is history, tomorrow is a mystery, and today is a gift. That's why it's called the present."

—ELEANOR ROOSEVELT

"Only when your consciousness is totally focused on the moment you are in, can you receive whatever gift, lesson, or delight that moment has to offer."

—BARBARA DEANGELIS

(AN INSPIRATIONAL AMERICAN SPEAKER AND AUTHOR.)

"Oops—there I go again."—my own personal creation! It's a quick, compassionate phrase that puts the brakes on thoughts that take you where you don't want to be.

We always have a choice in dealing with the present moment. We can either embrace it or resist it. Embracing the now doesn't mean that we necessarily like what is happening; it simply means that we acknowledge what is happening. When things "go wrong," and from time to time they certainly do, the act of embracing rather than resisting the now helps put us in a frame of mind that can help deal with the issue. Embracing the now can eliminate anger, despair and frustration. Embracing the now helps conjure up positive actions rather than destructive, negative ones. For example, accepting that your car won't start when you need to get to an appointment, will allow you to move quickly to a positive course of action that will solve your problem. Resisting the fact that your car won't start could cause anger and make you do something that might only compound your misery. The philosophy that I try to embrace is that no matter how bad the situation gets, as long as I can live to tell about it, things aren't that bad. I try to tell myself that at least I'll have a great story to tell. Notice and embrace the present moment and make the constructive choice!

Living in the present moment is being consciously aware of thoughts as they cross our minds. It means being aware of circumstances as they come our way.

Being in the present moment allows us to step back from each thought and situation and make the choice of how to deal with those circumstances in a way that enables us to fashion a life that is stress-free and brings us only joy and fulfillment.

44

Oops,—There You Go Again

Throughout this book I offer many ways to lighten up and to be a little happier. As much as you might find one or more of these ideas suited for you, they still require you to make some kind of change. And let's face it, happiness may be simple, but it is not always easy, especially when change is involved. One of the most important rules of thumb to remember is that you are the creator of your own experience. What you think about all day long determines your life. If you want to be happy, you are not going to get there if you are dwelling on negative thoughts, worrying about the past or the future or focusing on problems.

The first step is to begin to notice any unconstructive thoughts you may be holding on to. As you go about your daily activities, take a step back and observe yourself periodically. Just take notice—don't criticize or chastise yourself. Now you may be thinking, "How can I possibly monitor the thousands of thoughts that run through my mind daily?" You can't. But you do have a built-in alert system: your emotions. Your emotions will give you cues on whether you are working towards happiness or away from it. They are like automatic signals telling you the status of your well-being. Make it your daily intention to become more aware of what is going on in your mind and then notice what emotional state you find yourself in.

By hanging onto thoughts that disturb you, you will most likely wind up feeling stress, sadness or even depression. By being aware of your emotional state, you can catch yourself thinking thoughts that feel disempowering and then choose thoughts that feel better. Let your feelings be your barometer. If you notice

Happiness is a choice; it's that simple.

that you are ornery most of the time, what thoughts keep bringing you there? And if you are feeling really good, what were you paying attention to just before you noticed how good you felt?

How do you know if you are on the track toward simple happiness? You will always feel some sense of relief. Even if you go from sadness to anger to frustration to hope, you will always feel continued relief along the way.

So often, we don't pay attention to the power we have over our own sense of well-being. We just go with our feelings, assuming that we have no power over how we feel. The truth is that we are the only ones in the driver's seat. Unhappiness or happiness is a personal choice.

As I have said before, noticing and observing your feelings and preceding thoughts is the first step. The second step is to have a strategy for removing yourself from a downward spiral to shifting yourself to an upward swing. There is phrase I like to use called "Oops—there I go again," which I share here as a type of technique to keep your thoughts where you want them. Try this simple three-step approach:

1. Observe your negative feeling and take note of the thought that caused that feeling.

2. Step back in your mind and say to yourself, "Oops—there I go again."

3. Consciously let that negative thought go by bringing to mind thoughts of appreciation.

The next time you find yourself worrying or becoming stressed over the thoughts your mind entertains, simply hold out a mental stop sign by saying, "Oops—there I go again," and then conjure up some thoughts that make you feel good. You will be amazed at the power you have to not only change your thoughts, but your state of being and your entire life!

Happiness is a choice; it's that simple.

Reaching Higher

45

Be the Compassionate Observer of Yourself

Many of us often explain our actions by such phrases as "We're creatures of habit" or "That's the way I've always done it." These phrases indicate an attitude that, for better or worse, we're stuck in whatever place we find ourselves. We rationalize our behavior to justify our lot in life. Many of us are stuck in our comfort zone, hoping that some circumstance will come our way to light up our life, to give us a spark of joy and fulfillment.

We can sit back and wait or we can decide to move ahead. The decision is ours to make. Once we have made the decision to live a fuller, more joyful life, we need to begin to observe ourselves as we deal with the circumstances of our daily lives. By "observing," I mean just simply noticing our feelings and thoughts as they occur.

As you deal with circumstances, take notice of your emotional state. Ask yourself, "How do I feel right now?

Am I angry? Am I frustrated? Am I impatient? Am I relaxed? Am I pleased? Do I feel good or do I feel bad?" Noticing how you feel is the first step. Once you take note of how you feel, you can ask yourself, "Do I like how I feel?" and if you don't like how you feel then you might ask yourself, "How would I like to feel in this situation?"

By observing your life as it unfolds, you are truly living in the moment. This self-observation process leads you to begin to understand that maybe we're not "creatures of habit" but "creators by choice." As the observer, you can see that there is another way to look at any situation.

Some of us spend much of our time and energy observing and judging others. Why not transfer some of that energy to the only place that can really make a difference—to ourselves! You'll be amazed at what you notice!

Be the compassionate observer of yourself. Without judgment or criticism, simply observe yourself. As we develop our ability to rise above and take notice of our actions and resulting feelings, we begin to realize that we have options. We have choices that can lead to more satisfying actions and their resulting good feelings. In making higher choices, we surround ourselves with a comfortable, empowering aura that reveals to us the fact that we do have power over our lives!

What is Your Mission in Life?

Have you ever asked yourself the question, "What is my mission in life?" Maybe you have. In any event, here is another opportunity to consider this issue. Do you ever step back and consider the big picture? It's not always easy to do in today's hurried, multi-tasking world.

Are you always in a rush, feeling like you have more things to do than you have time to do them? Maybe you're a candidate for stopping for a moment, stepping out of the rat race and considering your mission in life. Once you understand what your mission in life is, things start to fall into place. You start to see the big picture, you gain perspective. You begin to realize that some things are more important than others. Finding your purpose can help you prioritize your activities, putting first things first. You can begin to focus on doing what is really important to you and forgetting about doing things just because someone else told you to do them.

I'm not here to tell you what your mission in life

should be or where to find it. What I am saying is that you have one. I am suggesting that if you don't understand that you have a purpose in life, you run the risk of one day finding yourself shaking your head, feeling unfulfilled and wondering where your life went.

Everyone is born into this world with a purpose. There is something that we are all uniquely qualified to achieve. How do you find out what your purpose is? The best way is to ask yourself and then spend some quiet time with the intention of letting the answer reveal itself to you. It may not come to you right away; it may evolve as you grow. Usually it has something to do with what you are good at or something that you enjoy doing. This is a good place to start. Ask yourself where your talents lie. Often, it is in realizing and cultivating our gifts that we find our purpose.

One of my favorite words is legacy. What do you want your legacy to be? What impact will your life have on those you love; those you work with? How many individuals will your life touch? Many people have found that their mission lies in giving their lives away to benefit others.

Once we understand what our mission in life is, then our life will have meaning and purpose no matter what our age. Richard Bach wrote, "Here's a test to determine whether or not your mission on earth is finished. If you're still breathing, it isn't."

47

Your Greatest Fear or Your Greatest Joy

In all my talks, the subject of why many people don't live the life of their dreams or follow their bliss always comes up. Most of my message is about being happier, living your life to its fullest. For some, this seems like a far reach. When I ask why, some say it's because they have too many responsibilities or just plain laziness. However, the majority of people in my audiences say it is fear. They say they don't follow their bliss for fear of the unknown, fear of failure and fear of rejection.

I'd like to share this amazing quotation that I cut out from my local newspaper several years ago and keep tucked in my desk blotter so I can refer to it often. Credit for the quote goes to Marianne Williamson from her work, A Return to Love: Reflections on the Principles of a Course in Miracles. Williamson writes: "Our deepest fear is not that we are inadequate. Our deepest fear is that we are powerful beyond measure. It is our light, not our darkness, that most frightens us. We ask ourselves, who am I to be brilliant, gorgeous, talented, fabulous…? Actually, who are you not to be? You are a child of God. Your playing small doesn't serve the world. There's nothing enlightened about shrinking so that other people won't feel insecure around you… We were born to make manifest the glory of God that is within us. It's not just in some of us; it's in everyone. And as we let our own light shine, we unconsciously give other people permission to do the same. As we're liberated from our own fear, our presence automatically liberates others."

Every sentence of that quote just knocks me out. It inspires me to reflect on my own fears and how I use my faith to overcome them. In my professional life, I have taken a few leaps of faith. For fourteen years, I was happily working in education. My routine was comfortable and I felt financially secure. Then one summer while working at a local tennis club, I started to think that maybe there was more for me out there. But leaving a secure job with a steady paycheck was very scary, as was starting a new career. At the time, I was considering becoming an independent financial advisor working on 100% commission. Then the big "What if…" questions came to mind. What if I don't get any clients? What if I can't make enough money to support my family? What if I'm not good at it? What if I fail? I almost didn't do it. But the thought of going out on my own and working independently felt good. So, fear and all, I stepped out of my comfort zone and took a chance…on me!

Here I am again, twenty more years down the line,

and I find myself crossing that same road—discovering there is still more to life for me. Being comfortable and steady is nice, but it's not the end-all place to be. There is always something more to reach for beyond what feels safe that ultimately offers tremendous rewards. My experience with volunteering has taken me from casually offering of my time to the community to realizing my new career path as a motivational speaker. In a sense, by facing my fears, I have come full circle and am now using my gift of teaching to its fullest potential. If you had asked me back then if I ever thought about writing an inspirational book or becoming a motivational speaker, the answer would have been an emphatic "no". But now I find that when new opportunities come my way, I feel the fear and then do it anyway.

Whenever we reach for our greater self, fear inevitably steps in the way. Fear is not who we are. It is a separate entity that lives only when we give it life. When we face it and move through it, then fear evaporates into the light of our true selves.

Consider this: Does your fear bring you closer to your dreams or keep you from them? The next time you want to try something new or make a change and don't do it because of fear, pay close attention! Is your fear valid or is it only cloaking the potential of your light? Being "born to make manifest the glory of God within" means allowing yourself to live your greatest joy... not your greatest fear!

48

Believe in Miracles

The Webster dictionary defines a miracle as "something wonderful; a wonder, a marvelous thing, something which seems to go beyond the known laws of nature and is held to be the act of a supernatural being; a supernatural event."

People have beliefs usually based upon their upbringing, culture, religion or by the influence of their parents and/or extended family. Apart from the belief in miracles, one might be left with a system of beliefs that has had, and will certainly continue to have, enormous significance—good and bad—in their lives. Not that all these inherited beliefs should be discarded, but only the falsity of their beliefs, which keep them from living a joyful, fulfilled life. If miracles are events which go beyond logical reason or scientific evidence and defy the laws of nature, then it can be understood that some of our beliefs are in things we may not fully understand or have not yet experienced with all our senses. Therefore, it might be a good idea to keep ourselves open to expand our belief systems and not just follow them blindly.

"Have a mind that's open to everything and attached to nothing," is a chapter in Wayne Dyer's book *10 Secrets to Success and Inner Peace*. In it, he discusses the fact that in order to grow, sometimes we have to let go of some beliefs and patterns of thought. New ideas foster growth and can give us a different perspective.

There is an interesting phenomenon called the "placebo effect" that occurs when drug companies test their new products. Usually two groups take a pill that is meant to help with a particular ailment. Unbeknownst to the participants, each group is given pills, but one group is given an

Allow yourself to expand the realm of possibilities.

active drug and the other is given *inactive* pills. An interesting result often occurs. A percentage of people who take the inactive pills respond as if they had taken the real thing. Just *believing* that they took a drug to help them was enough to achieve their desired outcome. It is obvious that there was no actual medicine that helped them; it was in the person's head. Nevertheless, just by believing, the participants made their healing happen. One might call that "a miracle!" It doesn't always occur, but there are enough case studies that prove it can.

You've probably also heard of people whose arthritic pain is relieved by wearing a copper bracelet, or by wearing a crystal necklace. Doctors and scientists are unable to explain this. Could it be that a magnetic field is created by the bracelet or necklace that causes the healing to occur, or is it just something that, as of now, we don't understand? Spontaneous healings have been going on for centuries with no true explanations. These too, can be, by definition, miracles.

We get so caught up in the scientific method that we lose sight of what we have not yet discovered. A majority of people hold a very skeptical attitude toward anything that can't be proven, based on what we know to be true. To me, this in itself is a limiting belief. Perhaps science hasn't caught up with all that is possible in the universe. It is certain that we still have much to learn and to unveil in this ever-expanding universe!

According to Napoleon Hill, the author of the classic book entitled, *Think and Grow Rich*, "What ever the mind of man can conceive and believe, it can achieve." So open your mind to the unknown. Don't act as though you know all the answers. Let go of your sophisticated attitude from time to time. Allow yourself to expand the realm of possibilities. Believe in yourself. Believe in others. Believe in miracles. They are lined up just waiting for you to allow them into your life.

49

Your Spiritual Side— You are Not Only Human

Have you ever checked out an acorn; the favorite nut of the squirrel? If you look at it closely, you can see that an acorn is greenish brown in color. It is cylindrical in shape with a point on the bottom and a cap on the top. If you cut into it, you'll see a fibrous material inside. It has its own physical characteristics. What would happen if you planted it in the middle of a field in a patch of cultivated earth? Chances are that over the years, it would grow into a giant oak tree.

Be honest, does an acorn in anyway resemble an oak tree? No, not at all! But somehow, it contains the "essence" of an oak tree; it has an unseen part I'll call "treeness." This concept, originated by author and inspirational speaker, Jean Houston, Ph.D., clarifies that even though we can't see it inside or out, an oak tree is still there waiting to be fully developed.

Using the acorn analogy as a type of comparison to human beings, you can then identify that humans, too, have an essence that is unseen. It is known as your "divineness;" or your "spirit;" or your "soul." You might say that we are made up of a physical body and a nonphysical soul. Like the potential "treeness" that exists in the acorn, your spiritual side can be fully realized if you understand that you are more than just human. Throughout your lifetime, you may or may not see your soul's latent abilities. Some know they are more than flesh, but live in an external, material world and ignore their soul's calling. It is not until they come closer to death, whether in old age, sickness, or a traumatic experience, that they begin to think about their soul's existence. In their perception of an end in sight, they wonder what will happen to their soul once they die. For those who have explored their spiritual side through religion, prayer or faith, they may feel a sense of peace about death. But I have found that even the most religious or spiritual people still feel an uncertainty about death and hope that there really is an afterlife waiting for them. Nevertheless, our soul's purpose is not about death, it is about eternal life.

Sometimes when faced with a seemingly insurmountable problem, we throw up our hands and say, "I'm only human!" When we separate ourselves from our spiritual side, and rely on only our human side or our ego, everything feels like a burden. We think, "Everything is up to me! It's me against everyone else! I have to protect what is mine from the world!" In our human side, we develop fears and hatreds. We take a defensive stance and build walls around us. Our life's challenges feel impossible to overcome.

The 20th century French theologian, Pierre Teilhard de Chardin, said, "We are not human beings having a spiritual experience. We are spiritual beings having a human experience." As we explore this spiritual side, we realize that we are not only human, but divine as well. Suddenly, there is light in places where there was once only darkness. Things start to change. We look at everything and everyone differently. What seemed impossible becomes possible. You see the divinity in others, that all people are really basically the same. Regardless of our race or religion, we all share the same divine essence. When we remember that all people are children of the same Creator, our fears and hatreds can begin to melt away. Our minds and hearts open with compassion. The walls around us crumble as we understand that each one of us is truly a spiritual being living a human experience.

Do you want to get to know your spiritual side? Like becoming familiar with anyone, you need to spend some time talking and listening. Prayer is your chance to talk to your spirit side and meditation is a quiet moment just for listening. Incorporate a daily practice of nurturing your soul with prayer and meditation. Be patient. As you become one with your divine self, higher thoughts will begin to appear—inspirations, innovative ideas, solutions to problems, a fresh look at an old issue—that also bring a sense of peace and joy. At first, the fresh stream of thoughts might feel foreign to you. "Are these really my thoughts?" you'll say. Soon you will feel comfortable with the realization that they are coming from your heart—your soul. These wonderful, insightful notions have always been there, waiting for you to give them a chance to enter your consciousness. Through meditation, as you are "in spirit," inspirations will come to you!

Cultivating your spiritual side is easy. It doesn't cost anything. You don't need any new equipment. No special clothing or posture is required. All that is necessary is the desire to connect with the part of you that is unseen. As a nurtured acorn grows to be a majestic tree, so too, will the human who fosters the soul transcend the physical body to become one with the Creator.

Unlock Your Power

Becoming a Little Happier

A number of years ago, I read a book by the prominent New York City psychologist, Albert Ellis, known as the Father of Rational Emotive Therapy, entitled *How to Make Yourself Happy, and Remarkably Less Disturbable.* In it, Ellis clearly suggests "happiness is a choice."

Wouldn't it be nice if everyday you could become a little happier, a little less "disturbable"? Well, you can! First, you must have the intention to do so. Then, the key is to be conscious of your feelings. Notice it when you are happy and notice it when you are disturbed. The happy part is easy. Awareness of your happiness plays an important role in choosing how you want to feel. The more difficult part is to be less disturbed at a moment that would usually cause you to be unhappy. The main ingredient here is how you choose to react in any a given situation. Understanding that you actually have a choice is not only an empowering notion, but a realistic tool in creating your desired state of being. The fact is, the reaction that you choose in any circumstance will always result in either your feeling happy, (good) or your feeling disturbed, (not so good).

While shopping at the supermarket one day, I decided to use the express line since I only had a few groceries. When I got there, the young man in front of me had only one item. Then I noticed that the woman ahead of him must have had 20 items or more. This seems to happen all too often at the express checkout line, which can be irritating to most people. As I was confronted with this situation, I could have gotten aggravated and expressed my displeasure to everyone around me. I might have even felt justified. After all, it seemed that the woman was being totally inconsiderate to those of us who had less than the maximum number of items for the express line. I also had the choice to be patient and compassionate with the woman. Perhaps she was a single mom trying to get her shopping done before having to pick up her kids at daycare, or maybe the clerk had turned on the express line sign after the woman had unloaded her wagon onto the counter. Whatever her reason, I was faced with the option to be disturbed and send out anger and hostility, or to choose compassion and send out love. In this case, I had chosen to be sympathetic, and as it turns out, the clerk had just changed the sign.

The bottom line is that your response to any situation is the main factor in determining whether you feel good or feel bad. The choice is always yours. For me, attempting to feel good no matter what is going on around me is a personal choice. When I saw the woman had more than the limit, my initial reaction was to be annoyed. Then I thought, "Is waiting another two or three minutes really going to matter?" By changing my view first, it helped me to be more patient. At that moment, I felt better, which made it easier for me to send out love.

Realize that your reaction can lead you either way. It's not necessarily the circumstances in your life that makes you happy or disturbed; it is how you deal with them. When you start choosing the reaction that leads you to being "a little happier, a little less disturbable," your life will be just that!

51

Don't Die with
Your Music Still in You

In Wayne Dyer's book entitled, *10 Secrets to Success and Inner Peace*, one of his secrets is, "Don't die with your music still in you." The word music is used as a metaphor for any gift or talent that we may possess. In keeping with a musical image, you can envision that everyone holds their own unique melody within, a melody which is waiting to be tuned into. Many go through their entire life searching for harmony from the outside world and never pursue their own inner song waiting to be sung. It is up to each of us to tap into our own potential.

One key characteristic of happy people is that they know what makes them happy and they do it! When I ask my audiences, "Who has a hobby or activity they really love to do?" their faces give the best answer. Many faces immediately light up while others show a sinking expression. Some people know what makes them happy. Others aren't always quite sure. It is not that they don't have a gift; they just might not know that they do. Sometimes we know the things we are good at, yet for some reason, we don't utilize these talents. Though it is best to willingly explore your gifts, it often takes a life changing event to awaken the music within.

One of my neighbors was reaching the landmark birthday of 40 when he decided that he had no intention of being old and overweight. He realized that he could do nothing about the old part, but could make the overweight part his business. After beginning a regular a jogging program, he discovered he enjoyed it tremendously. Not only did he drop the weight, he also realized that he had more endurance and speed than he had initially realized. A plan to lose some weight turned into a daily training session for a local race. To his delight, he finished the 10K run with an average time of 6:48 per mile. That was good enough for 118th place in a world-class field of over 4,500. Not bad for someone who once thought himself old and fat! Today he continues to enjoy his training and will undoubtedly lower his time in next year's race. The point is that if you find something that you love, something that brings you joy when you are doing it, that's your music!

I believe we are all here on earth to enjoy our special abilities, whether privately or shared with the world. There's no reason to lead a life of quiet desperation. Are you living your music? Are you realizing your fullest potential? Is there something you've always wanted to do and haven't done it yet? What are your talents? Is it painting, writing, singing or dancing? Do you love gardening, building something, reading books? Is compassion your gift? Are you a teacher, a coach, a motivator? Seek out the music within. No more excuses. You have plenty of time and you are never too old to start.

Here's a joke to consider: An older woman says to her friend, "Do you know how old I'll be by the time I learn to play the piano?" Her insightful friend replies, "You'll be just as old as you'd be if you don't learn how to play the piano."

I offer four axioms about life and aging. I challenge you to commit them to memory and bring them to mind often:

1. The definition of old age is when regrets take the place of dreams.

2. As people age, they don't regret what they did in their lives; they regret the things they didn't do.

3. Few people on their death beds say, "I wish I had spent more time at the office"

4. This life is not a dress rehearsal; now is the only time you've got!

As Dyer so poignantly suggests, "Don't die with you music still in you." Get it out there, let your light shine, and dance to the beat of your heart!

Start to Live "Heaven on Earth"

As I began writing this book, the thought of fifty-two chapters kept coming to mind. I realized that each chapter unfolded as snippets of my ideas about living a happier life. It seemed logical that one might want to meditate or work on one chapter a week for a year. As I came closer to the end, I had some struggle as to what would be the final chapter. Initially, I decided it would be "Living in the Present Moment." So then my challenge was choosing which theme I would use for chapter fifty-one.

As I reviewed possible topics and what I had already written, I realized that all the ideas presented in this little book were leading in one direction. They represented all of the ways in which I endeavor each day to live the life of my dreams—a life full of joy and fulfillment. It became clear to me that I would end my book on that final thought.

This kind of life has been described to me in several different books I've read. Wayne Dyer's *The Power of*

Intention, Ester and Jerry Hicks' *Ask and it is Given* and Eckhart Tolle's *The Power of Now* all refer to a connection with our Divine Source. Does the realization and cultivation of this relationship with our Creator come first or is it the human practice of the concepts described in this book that lead us to understand that divine connection? My final conclusion is that it doesn't really matter; they go hand in hand. It became apparent to me that regardless of how we do it, connecting with our Divine Source is the only successful way to find true joy and happiness.

When I was a youngster, heaven was explained to me as a place where I would go after I died, if I was good. I was told that in heaven I would enjoy the "beatific vision" and be completely happy gazing on the "face of God." To be honest, I've always felt a little let down by that description of Heaven. For a little kid, and even for an adult, it seemed that there should be a better reward than that.

> *We can choose every aspect of our lives...*

However, I have to admit, as I attempt to live the principles that I have shared in this book, I get little glimpses—feelings of such intense joy—that I wonder how there could be anything better. There is a feeling I get of oneness with my Creator, a feeling ever so fleeting, but one that is undeniable. I experience the unconditional love that is constantly being showered down on me and everyone else who walks on this earth. These blissful moments usually come when I'm living in my purpose and giving of myself to others. They occur when I'm able to send out love even when love is not being sent my way. They happen when I am fortunate enough to share in the experience of the unconditional love of another. It sounds a bit mystical, and it may be, but I feel that these are insights into what heaven is really like. I also believe that this kind of joyful experience is available, not only in quick peeks, but fully to anyone willing to allow our Creator's goodness to flow into his or her life.

I get shivers up and down my spine when I hear the words from James Taylor's song, "Carry me on my Way." These lines really sum up the message: "I forget what to ask for, there isn't anything I haven't been given. How could I wish for anything more as I am here living in heaven?"

It's here for all of us to discover. As humans, we have the gift of "free-will." We can choose every aspect of our lives—good or bad. To seek a life filled with joy, and the unlimited stream of unconditional love available to us, we truly begin to experience "Heaven on Earth!"

About the Author

Motivational speaker and author, Jim Ryan, continued pursuing his passion for teaching after receiving his Masters in Guidance and Counseling from Queens College, Flushing, New York. After 14 years of counseling and teaching French and Italian to middle school students, Jim decided to shift his interpersonal skills to the business sector. An Independent Financial Planner for over 22 years, a longstanding member of Rotary International and past-president of The Northport Rotary Club, he serves many in his hometown community of Northport, New York. He was "Man of the Year in Civics" in 2005 from the *The Times of Northport* and is a graduate of "Leadership Huntington," a highly recognized program offered by the *Huntington Chamber Foundation*.

In February of 2000, Jim took an opportunity to give back to his community in a different way by volunteering in his local prison system, teaching a course in personal development. The success of the program set off a chain of events that prompted Jim to create several powerful motivational talks and inspired him to author his book, *Simple Happiness: 52 Easy Ways to Lighten Up.*

Jim continues his motivational speaking career, having already inspired thousands, by sharing his **Simple Happiness** message, **"You can live your best life now."**

With his wit, candor, songs and anecdotes, Jim has a unique ability to turn profound, life-changing concepts into easily understood solutions that reach the heart of his audiences. He has been a guest on several radio programs, featured in *Long Island Business News* and appeared on the cable television show *The God Squad,* with nationally acclaimed co-hosts Father Tom and Rabbi Gellman.

For information about Jim's motivational programs, or to comment on his book, please contact Jim Ryan Talks at 866-JIM-RYAN or visit his website at: **www.JimRyanTalks.com**.

393

Printed in the United States
69137LVS00001B/97-150